# CRIME
# AND
# PUNISHMENT

*A Mind to Murder*

TWAYNE'S MASTERWORK STUDIES
*Robert Lecker, General Editor*

# CRIME AND PUNISHMENT

## A Mind to Murder

### GARY COX

TWAYNE PUBLISHERS • BOSTON
*A Division of G. K. Hall & Co.*

*Crime and Punishment: A Mind to Murder*
Gary Cox

Twayne's Masterwork Studies No. 45

Copyright 1990 by G. K. Hall & Co.
All rights reserved.
Published by Twayne Publishers
A Division of G. K. Hall & Co.
70 Lincoln Street, Boston, Massachusetts   02111

Copyediting supervised by Barbara Sutton
Book production by Janet Z. Reynolds
Typeset in 10/14 Sabon by Compset, Inc., Beverly, Massachusetts

Printed on permanent/durable acid-free paper
and bound in the United States of America

Library of Congress Cataloging-in-Publication Data

Cox, Gary.
    Crime and punishment : a mind to murder / Gary Cox.
        p.   cm.—(Twayne's masterwork studies ; no. 45)
    Includes bibliographical references.
    ISBN 0-8057-7993-0 (alk. paper).—ISBN 0-8057-8042-4 (pbk. :alk. paper)
    1.  Dostoyevsky, Fyodor, 1821–1881.   Prestuplenie i nakazanie.
  I. Title.   II.  Series.
    PG3325.P73C68   1990                                          89-38929
    891.73'3—dc20                                                 CIP

First published 1990.
10 9 8 7 6 5 4 3 2 1 (alk. paper)
10 9 8 7 6 5 4 3 2 1 (pbk. :alk. paper)

# Contents

# Note on the References
# and Acknowledgments

*Books in Print* lists fourteen English editions of *Crime and Punishment* (one of which is offered with a "student activity book" and another is in comic book format); most of these are editions of the translations made by Constance Garnett and Jessie Coulson. These are both superb translations and have been around for a long time (in some cases, editors have corrected occasional euphemisms, errors, and dated phraseology but have left the Garnett and Coulson texts basically intact). Other available editions are translated by David Magarshack and Sidney Monas; these are both fine translations. A Soviet-produced edition is ably translated by Julius Katzer. It is wise to stay away from editions that do not mention the name of the translator.

The Russian language is written with a non-Latin alphabet, called Cyrillic (after Saint Cyril, who is said to have invented it). Various systems are used for transcribing Russian into Latin letters. The system used here is popular rather than scholarly. This means that it is less precise than a scholarly system but precise enough for our purpose. It avoids those exotic diacritical marks that can make technical transcription systems so intimidating and confusing.

## Note on the References and Acknowledgments

Russian names are given in their Russian, not their Westernized, forms (for example, "Nikolai," not "Nicholas"; "Konstantin," not "Constantine"; "Fyodor," not "Theodore") with two exceptions: this book uses "Alexander" (not "Aleksandr") and Peter (not "Pyotr"). (The Bibliography also contains exceptions: it presents names in the forms used by the books in question, so that Nikolai Berdyaev, for instance, appears as "Nicholas Berdyaev," because that is the form of his name used by his publishers.) German names (and this novel has many Russified Germans in it) appear in their original German form, not in transcribed Russian (e.g., "Koch," not "Kokh"; "Resslich," not "Resslikh"; "Ludwigovna," not "Lyudvigovna"). Feminine name endings are dropped, and all names, even of women, are presented in masculine form (e.g., "Dunya Raskolnikov," not "Dunya Raskolnikova"; "Sonya Marmeladov," not "Sonya Marmeladova"). Note also that endings in *-ii* are given as *-y* (e.g., "Dostoevsky," not "Dostoevskii"); also, when Russian *e* is pronounced *yo*, in this book it is spelled that way (e.g., "Alyona," not "Alena"; "Fyodor," not "Fedor"), even when this is a departure from standard usage.

Thanks are due to Dedman College of Southern Methodist University for offering leave of absence from teaching duties during the spring 1988 semester, to Jo Fay Godbey's University Lecture Series at SMU for offering me the opportunity to give a series of lectures on this novel as I was beginning my work, to Peggy Billo for her helpful comments on the manuscript, and to my students at SMU who have helped me work out these ideas through the years. I would also like to thank Professor Nadine Natov of the North American Dostoevsky Society for making it possible for me to give a talk based on these materials entitled "Rhyming Character Triangles in *Crime and Punishment* as an Instance of 'Spatial Form'" at the International Dostoevsky Symposium in Ljubljana, Yugoslavia, 23–28, July 1989.

Fyodor M. Dostoevsky
Photograph, 1860s

# Chronology: Fyodor Dostoevsky's Life and Works

| | |
|---|---|
| 1821 | Dostoevsky born to military doctor (with ancestry in clergy) and merchant's daughter, in Moscow, where father works at the Mariinsky (Saint Mary's) Hospital for the poor. |
| 1828 | Dostoevsky's father promoted to "collegiate assessor" rank, entitling him to privileges of hereditary nobility; enters Fyodor and one-year-older brother Mikhail on rolls of nobility. |
| 1831 | Dostoevsky family purchases small estate near Moscow. Dostoevsky witnesses production of Schiller's *The Robbers*. |
| 1832 | Family goes into debt to purchase neighboring village. |
| 1833 | Reads Walter Scott during summer. |
| 1834 | The brothers enter prestigious boarding school for boys in Moscow. |
| 1837 | Pushkin dies. Dostoevsky's mother dies after prolonged illness. The brothers travel to St. Petersburg and enter prestigious Academy of Military Engineers, characterized by harsh hazing and a student body made up of socioeconomic climbers, with little interest in the arts. |
| 1837–1839 | Friendship with Ivan Shidlovsky, an expansive and contradictory "romantic nature," an important mentor for both boys. |
| 1838 | Reads E. T. A. Hoffmann and Balzac. |
| 1839 | Dostoevsky's father murdered by his own serfs, when peasant unrest sweeps region. |

1840        Rhapsodizes over Victor Hugo in letter to brother.

1841        Receives commission; moves to apartment; spends money un-
            wisely; writes, but does not finish, plays.

1842        Gogol's *Dead Souls* and "The Overcoat" published; Belinsky
            hails them as masterpieces of social criticism; birth of "Natu-
            ral School."

1843        Dostoevsky graduates from Academy; goes to work in draft-
            ing department of St. Petersburg Engineering Command.

1844        Dostoevsky's translation of Balzac's *Eugenie Grandet*
            published.

1845        Dostoevsky completes *Poor Folk*, a "natural school" piece—
            that is, a sentimental depiction of the hard lot of the urban
            poor; it is shown to several major critics, among them Belin-
            sky, who raves about it; Dostoevsky becomes a major writer
            overnight.

1846        Dostoevsky's second novella, *The Double*, a Gothic fantasy
            with roots in Gogolian humor, but with complex psychologi-
            cal implications, is poorly received. Dostoevsky's excitable
            vanity makes him a butt of jokes among Belinsky's inner circle;
            Turgenev and Nekrasov publish poem lampooning him. In-
            volvement with moderate utopian socialist Beketov circle.
            Mild epilepsy diagnosed.

1847        *The Landlady*, a Hoffmannesque Gothic, published; Belinsky
            becomes disaffected with Dostoevsky's work.

1848        Uprisings in Western Europe; excitement among Petersburg
            intellectuals; attendance increases at Petrashevsky's Friday so-
            cialist study group; Dostoevsky begins attending regularly. Be-
            linsky dies.

1849        Dostoevsky becomes involved in Speshnyov's radical activist
            group within Petrashevsky circle, which plans to acquire print-
            ing press and disseminate propaganda on emancipation of
            serfs. Dostoevsky arrested and imprisoned in Peter and Paul
            Fortress. Sentenced to death; suffers mock execution with last
            minute commutation (as planned, for effect) by Nikolai I.

1850–1854   In prison in Omsk (southwestern Siberia); reads *New
            Testament*.

1853–1855   Crimean War.

1854        Dostoevsky released from prison; required to serve as low-
            ranking military engineer in Semipalatinsk, Siberia. Begins
            lifelong friendship with Baron A. E. Wrangel, then a young

|  | public prosecutor in Semipalatinsk, later a major public figure in the development of Siberia. |
|---|---|
| 1855 | Nikolai I dies; Alexander II accedes to throne, planning emancipation and other reforms. |
| 1857 | Dostoevsky marries Maria Isaev in Semipalatinsk. Publishes "A Little Hero" without signature. |
| 1859 | Humorous pieces *Uncle's Dream* and *The Village of Stepanchikovo* (first translated into English as *A Friend of the Family*) published. Dostoevsky receives permission to return to European Russia. |
| 1860 | Dostoevsky returns to St. Petersburg and renews ties with progressive friends. Early chapters of prison memoirs published. |
| 1861 | Dostoevsky and brother Mikhail found journal *Time*, with idea (called "soil-ism" [*pochvennichestvo*]) of bridging chasm between educated classes and common people, and thus between Slavophiles and Westernizers. *The Insulted and the Injured* published. |
| 1862 | Turgenev's *Fathers and Sons*, with controversial portrayal of young radical, published. Unrest on left; fires in city blamed on radicals; Chernyshevsky and others arrested; Chernyshevsky writes *What Is to Be Done?* in prison, as answer to Turgenev. Dostoevsky travels to Western Europe; experiences provide material for travel essays, *Winter Notes on Summer Impressions*. Prison memoirs, *Notes from the House of the Dead*, published. |
| 1863 | Uprising in Poland, against Russian hegemony, becomes issue for Russian left; *Time* closed because of ambiguous piece on this question. Dostoevsky travels to Europe with Polina Suslov, an emancipated young woman who treats him abominably. He gambles compulsively; borrows money from Turgenev. |
| 1864 | Dostoevsky brothers publish new journal, *Epoch*. Dostoevsky's wife Maria dies of consumption. Mikhail Dostoevsky dies. *Notes from Underground*, a parody of *What Is to Be Done?* and an exposition of Dostoevsky's mature view of human predicament, published in *Epoch*. |
| 1865 | *Epoch* fails for financial reasons. Dostoevsky's financial woes compounded by support of late wife's family, gambling, debts, travels (chasing Suslov again), disastrous agreements with unscrupulous publishers. Working on *The Drunkards*, later incorporated as the Marmeladov subplot of *Crime and Punishment*, which is accepted in advance for serial publication in Katkov's the *Russian Messenger*. |

doubt, religious knowledge, guilt, and redemption. Shares honors with *Crime and Punishment* as Dostoevsky's greatest novels.

1881    Dostoevsky dies. Alexander II assassinated by left-wing terrorists.

# 1

# Historical Context

Dostoevsky was certainly a man of his age, but just as certainly he transcended it. Like his great contemporary, Tolstoy, he took the issues he found current and built from them a world so completely his own that it seems scarcely recognizable. Dostoevsky's novelistic world is a distinctly Russian one, even a distillation of all that is Russian, yet its issues become so profoundly universal that it rises above its surroundings.

Dostoevsky began where many of his contemporaries did—as a member of the nascent left-wing intelligentsia of the 1840s. But in the course of his career he moved in an opposite direction. It is not just that he became more conservative, although he eventually did. But his view of the human personality took on a depth and complexity that left his contemporaries, liberal or conservative, in the dust. We must look at Dostoevsky's intellectual surroundings; they provide the building blocks of his world, however he may have transcended them.

In 1825, when Dostoevsky was five years old, Alexander I died and a group of officers staged an unsuccessful coup d'état to establish a constitutional monarchy. Alexander had come to power a quarter of a century earlier with heady ideas of reform and constitutional government, but in the course of his reign he had lost interest, what with Napoleonic wars, international politics, the influence of conservative advisors, and his own growing religious mysticism. The young officers (later called Decembrists, since their attempted coup took place in December) were frustrated when reforms did not materialize. Scions of the nobility, holding rank as officers in the army (that was simply what young noblemen did at the time), they had received the best education money and influence could buy in that time and place, which meant, of course, that they read Voltaire, Rousseau, Diderot, and the like. They persuaded their soldiers to march onto the square and demand "Konstantin and a constitution." Their uprising was easily put down, the ringleaders either hanged or sent to Siberian prison and exile, and Nikolai I, the conservative younger brother of the more liberal Konstantin, ascended to the throne.

Nikolai would have been a reactionary in any case, but the failed uprising gave him a special reason for taking repressive measures. And he certainly did. The minister of culture, Uvarov, demanded allegiance to the slogan of "autocracy, orthodoxy, nationality," while Count Beckendorff, the head of the secret police, enforced a policy of cultural orthodoxy.

The three decades that followed, dominated by Nikolai's repressive regime, saw the development and solidification of the major features of Russian intellectual culture. Russian culture came of age during these decades and created the outline for its own sense of identity. Russia's first world-class authors, Pushkin, Lermontov, and Gogol, created all or a major portion of their works during this period. Russia's first great literary critic, Belinsky, laid down the principles of an engagé literature that have become all but canonical in the Russian tradition. Universities grew in size and importance, despite the fact that Uvarov and Beckendorff viewed them as subversive organizations. And Russia's greatest writers of fiction, Dostoevsky among them, came to maturity and began their writing careers during this period.

The pressure-cooker atmosphere of Russian intellectual culture under Nikolai was an ideal environment for the importation and propagation of the idealistic philosophy that was a part of German romanticism. The doctrines of Schelling and Hegel, with their emphasis on the greater reality of the life of the mind over the paraphernalia of the physical world, took hold rapidly among Russian intellectuals of the 1830s, for they did indeed feel that the ideas that could only be discussed in the semisecret literary circle (*kruzhók*) or salon were more real than the banality of public life under Nikolai. And the romantic emphasis on the discovery of national identity and the role of one's own nation in the progress of universal spirit appealed to Russian thinkers intent on discovering those very things.

But when they took a hard look at their own culture, they were often discouraged by what they did, or rather did not, find there. They became acutely aware of their own backwardness and their country's failure to contribute to European culture. Two major groups emerged in response to this problem: the Slavophiles and the Westernizers. The names are self-explanatory: as in any developing nation experiencing anxiety over its encounter with the developed world, one group becomes defensive, immerses itself in the indigenous culture, and asserts that it is not only equal but superior to the proud and decadent West, while the other seeks to assimilate the more advanced culture and looks to the future for any indigenous contribution. Arguments between the Slavophiles and the Westernizers dominated the late 1830s and early 1840s, but variations on this theme continued to be debated throughout Dostoevsky's lifetime and, indeed, down to the present day.

Belinsky was in the Westernizers' camp. It was he who established the principles of radical reformist criticism that were later taken up by Dostoevsky's contemporaries. For Belinsky, literature should be a forum for the discussion of social issues that could not be taken up directly in a repressive society. He said that literature should be realistic, the better to expose the social evils requiring reform. And he saw literary criticism as the queen of the sciences, its role being that of guide on matters social, political, and philosophical, as well as aesthetic. It was Belinsky who vaulted Dostoevsky to fame by praising his first novel, *Poor Folk*, as precisely the kind of social exposé he liked to see in literature, only to voice disappointment in his protégé's second novel, a psychological phantasmagoria called *The Double*. And it was Belinsky who wrote an outraged letter to Gogol (calling him a traitor to the cause of reform) that Dostoevsky read publicly in a left-wing salon—this action was one of the charges against him when he was arrested in 1849.

Dostoevsky's arrest resulted from his involvement with the Petrashevsky circle, a group that represented a significant shift in the intellectual life of the 1840s. German idealism was still present as a basis for thought, but French utopian socialism was the new rage. It was the work of Fourier and Saint-Simon that the Petrashevsky group studied and disseminated. In the aftermath of the 1848 uprisings in Western Europe (two well-known Russian intellectuals, Herzen and Bakunin, had participated), Nikolai wanted to prevent such uprisings from occurring in Russia by making an example of someone. Members of Petrashevsky's group were rounded up, Dostoevsky and others were imprisoned in the Peter and Paul Fortress, and in 1850 Dostoevsky was sent to work in Siberia.

The decade of the 1850s was one of quiet anticipation on the Russian intellectual and literary scene. Everyone knew that Nikolai would die soon, that the humiliating debacle of the Crimean War would end with his death, and most important, that the heir apparent, Alexander II, was planning reforms, this time for real. The most important reform was to be the abolition of serfdom, which was seen, first, as a great injustice, and second, as the greatest obstacle to the establishment of a modern government, characterized by both reason and conscience, in Russia. The title of one of Turgenev's novels, *On the Eve* (1860), expresses the sense of expectation that hovered over the Russian public at this time.

A group of radical leftist literary critics, following the late Belinsky (who died in 1848, just before Dostoevsky's arrest), was regrouping at the journal the *Contemporary*, led by such young theorists as Chernyshevsky, Dobrolyubov, and Pisarev. While they echoed Belinsky's ideas about the role of literature as social critique, their European gurus had changed—they scorned the lofty idealism of the 1830s and

1840s and turned to positivists and utilitarians like Comte, Bücher, and J. S. Mill, who wanted to use a scientific model for viewing society. Their social profile demonstrates an interesting shift. They came from various non-noble classes (the term *raznochintsy*, "people of various ranks," is often applied to them): some were disillusioned seminarians (both Chernyshevsky and Dobrolyubov, for instance); many were medical students; women played an unprecedented role in the movement. The growth of the universities (and a new policy: the admission of women to academic programs, particularly in medicine and midwifery) had much to do with these shifts. In any case, the new generation viewed society using a materialistic, a scientific, and even a medical model: society was an organism, Russian society a very sick one, but one that could be cured by the application of proper treatments.

The most outstanding representative of this generation was a fictional character, Turgenev's Bazarov, in *Fathers and Sons*. Turgenev's novels of the late 1850s provide marvelous documentation of the various social types of the period; the best of them is *Fathers and Sons*, which depicts the tensions between the idealists of the 1840s and the materialists of the 1860s with touching artistry. Bazarov is a young doctor, the son of a military doctor with low-level aristocratic status, an aggressively intelligent, brash Young Turk who accepts no authority, and who believes that the features of contemporary society must be destroyed before the new rational society can be built.

Bazarov gladly accepts the term *nihilist* (from the Latin *nihil*, "nothing"), which is coined with reference to him. The term is now in general usage to refer to this group, but it must be qualified. First, this group has absolutely nothing in common with the protoexistentialist "nihilists" of the late nineteenth and early twentieth centuries. Second, they were not believers in nothing—they simply said (incorrectly) that they accepted no authority and that the present must be destroyed to make way for the future. They were actually optimistic rationalists who believed passionately that the good society could be created by the reeducation of the masses according to scientific principles. The term *nihilist* cannot be avoided in reference to these thinkers—its usage is too general. But one ought to remember that it is fundamentally a misnomer. *Fathers and Sons* was received with passionate polemic by both sides of the issue, and the "rebuttal" from the nihilists took the form of another novel, this one by Chernyshevsky.

Although the long-awaited emancipation had finally occurred in 1861, serious problems came with it, and the young nihilists had grown more restless than ever. A series of fires in 1862 in St. Petersburg was (rightly or wrongly) attributed to them. Some "ringleaders," among them Chernyshevsky, were rounded up and interned in the Peter and Paul Fortress. There Chernyshevsky wrote the novel *What Is to Be Done?*, an ungainly concoction attempting to present the positive side of the "new people," the nihilists. It was the answer to *Fathers and Sons*.

Dostoevsky had been allowed to return from Siberia in the meantime, and was working as a journalist in St. Petersburg. The dating of Dostoevsky's turn toward conservative politics is a controversial issue. The received opinion has been that he turned conservative with his study of the New Testament in prison, but new evidence suggests that he was, in the early 1860s, still quite sympathetic to some of the goals of the Left but very impatient with their naively aggressive methods. In any case, he penned the third entry in this literary polemic, *Notes from Underground*—a devastating parody of *What Is to Be Done?* that raises the issues of the debate to a new level of philosophical and literary brilliance. It lampoons the utilitarian ethical syllogism by carrying it to a contradictory conclusion. The nihilists argued that man will be good once he learns that his own personal advantage coincides with the social good. The underground man objects that this theory turns a man into a dehumanized "piano key," and points out that the "advantage" man yearns for above everything else is freedom. But if he acts only according to his "advantage," he remains in a deterministic circle of logical behavior; to prove his freedom he must act illogically and counter to his own best interests, and as if to illustrate this, the underground man courts self-destruction with perverse glee. Barely noticed by contemporaries, the work does much more than lampoon Chernyshevsky. It lays out a new map of the human personality, with irrational drives bubbling beneath the surface of behavior, and it outlines Dostoevsky's view of the fundamental problem in human interaction: the inability to interact with others except through domination. Each of the large novels of Dostoevsky's mature years may be seen as an attempt to resolve this problem.

This sets the stage for the writing of *Crime and Punishment* (1866). It appeared that the nihilists had calmed down by this time—actually they had begun to go underground and to turn toward the terrorism that was to characterize them later on. Dostoevsky's own life was exceedingly tumultuous during the mid-1860s, but things calmed down with his marriage in 1867. He depicted the nihilists with increasing amounts of vitriol in the later novels *The Idiot* and *The Devils* (sometimes translated under the title *The Possessed*), and by 1873 he was writing for a reactionary journal. The new version of Slavophilism during the 1870s was pan-Slavism, which argued that it was Russia's destiny to dominate the Slavic peoples. Dostoevsky banged the pan-Slavic drum gleefully, in connection with the 1877–78 wars to liberate the Slavic Balkans from Turkish rule.

In 1881, only months after the publication of *The Brothers Karamazov*, and Dostoevsky's death, left-wing terrorists assassinated Alexander II, the tsar-liberator, and Russia's descent along the slippery slope toward revolution became inexorable.

# 2

# The Importance of the Work

How many times shall this our lofty scene be acted o'er, in states unborn and accents yet unknown?

—Shakespeare, *Julius Caesar*

One of the most extraordinary things about *Crime and Punishment*, and about Dostoevsky's work generally, is the fact that it appeals to readers from such a wide spectrum of political and religious thought, even from perspectives quite opposed to those of the author. It is a mystery that liberals, socialists, atheists, Jews, Poles, and Jesuits have been passionately devoted to Dostoevsky's work, despite the fact that he was hostile to the first two groups, at variance with the third, and downright bigoted toward the last three. How can thinkers so averse to his ideas be enthralled by their novelistic clothing?

One reason is that Dostoevsky depicted with brilliant concentration some of the most disturbing features of modern man's predicament. Indeed, he anticipated several of them. Both Sigmund Freud and Friedrich Nietzsche, whose careers overlapped Dostoevsky's, formulated their basic ideas before reading him, but discovered in Dostoevsky an anticipation of major elements of their work.

Second, while it is always clear where Dostoevsky stands on the issues he presents, he allows opposing voices to speak with real credibility, and often with tragic elevation. One important school of Dostoevsky criticism speaks of the "polyphonic," or "multivoiced" nature of his novels, his ability to engage opposing points of view in equally weighted dialogue. In fact, the opposed viewpoints are never allowed to be truly equal, but Dostoevsky certainly understood and expressed the pathos of his adversaries. And his artistic integrity would never permit him to stack the deck completely in his own favor. This is why D. H. Lawrence could accept everything in *Crime and Punishment* but its ending, and could argue that the Inquisitor, rather than Christ, is the moral victor in the "Legend of the Grand Inquisitor" chapter of *The Brothers Karamazov*. That is why Albert Camus could explore, in *The Stranger*, a character very like Raskolnikov except for his failure to achieve ultimate redemption. For some readers Dostoevsky poses the problems of alienation so powerfully that the answers he arrives at fail to satisfy. Others, of course, are satisfied, and for them Dostoevsky is not only an artist but a prophet.

Finally, Dostoevsky presents issues with such intensity that the very act of working through an idea with him often becomes an overwhelming experience. For some readers this is a drawback—not everyone likes to be overwhelmed. One tends to love Dostoevsky or hate him; there is little middle ground. On whichever side of the issue one ends up after reading Dostoevsky, one knows one has wrestled mightily with an idea.

What, then, are the great ideas that Dostoevsky wrestles with? Dostoevsky's world takes for granted a view of the personality that is really quite new, a new map of the mind and its relationship to action. For Dostoevsky, behavior is conditioned not so much by rational acts of will as by unconscious, irrational drives. This theory does not seem to be particularly conscious on the author's part; it is simply the way he sees and describes the thought and behavior of human beings. It is a view of life rooted in romanticism but propelled by alienation into modernism. And it is fundamentally the map we use today. The mind for Dostoevsky is not a set of rational constructs, but a living organism, subject to instincts and desires like any other organism, yet willing to sacrifice everything to be free.

Freud would develop and codify this new view of the personality, but he acknowledged that all of his work was already implicit in Dostoevsky's. And whether or not we are Freudians as such, we must all admit that the ideas of the mind current today owe much of their shape to what Freud described, and to what Dostoevsky, before him, implied.

Equipped with this new map of the mind, Dostoevsky has his extraordinary characters take a look at some of the major questions of human consciousness: the ethics of utility, the importance and structure of aggression in the human personality, the problem of political power, the existence of God, the nature of religious knowledge, the possibility of true and effective goodness in the human personality, the meaning of sex and love, the mechanisms of personal and family interaction, the alienation of man from his fellows. Again and again Dostoevsky's treatment of these issues becomes a prescient foreshadowing of the twentieth century. How many times has Raskolnikov's act been carried out, apparently for much the same reasons, during the twentieth century? And might not the microbe dream from the epilogue be the century's epigraph, or its epitaph?

There are also literary reasons for the continuing importance of Crime and Punishment, although, as in any work of Russian fiction, the intellectual elements constantly threaten to upstage the literary ones. The technique here called "situation rhyme" is a forerunner of literary modernism. And the work broke new ground in presenting a new kind of hero or protagonist, an antihero, although a closer look shows that the criminal protagonist of Crime and Punishment had substantial antecedents in Dostoevsky's own early work, and more important, in romanticism generally. Basically, Dostoevsky took elements of the cynical, yet introspective, Byronic hero (already explored perceptively in Russian flesh by Pushkin and Lermontov), fused it with the demonic heroism of spooky Gothic novels, and placed him in the urban slums of a Dickens, a Balzac, a Gogol. The product was a hero who represented an intensely thinking subject working through a moral or metaphysical problem with the reader. Elements of dialogue are heightened, not only between characters but between the work and its reader.

*Crime and Punishment* represents not only a new kind of hero but a new kind of fiction. It is a detective story, to be sure (although the genre barely existed), but one that focuses on the mental life of the criminal and his duel with a redemptive prosecutor. Thus the plot structure of *Crime and Punishment* was likewise an innovation.

Dostoevsky has had extraordinary impact on the writers of the twentieth century. The cosmos is divided between Tolstoy and Dostoevsky, said Lev Shestov, and this opposition has been echoed by Isaiah Berlin among others. Generally readers tend to gravitate toward one or the other, not toward both, and writers tend to take their cue either from Tolstoy's panoramic breadth or Dostoevsky's psychological depth, not from both. E. M. Forster said it was a "prophetic" character that distinguished Dostoevsky from a writer like Tolstoy, and Isaiah Berlin quoted Greek poet Archilochus to express the difference: "the fox knows many things, but the hedgehog knows the one important thing." Tolstoy is the clever fox for Berlin, Dostoevsky the wise hedgehog. Many twentieth-century writers may be placed, stylistically or ideologically, in the Dostoevskian camp. Dostoevsky's influence on Lawrence, Sartre, Camus, and Malraux has already been mentioned. Different writers have reacted to different works. Thus, it is hard to imagine Faulkner's steamy depictions of the lives of decaying rural nobility without *The Brothers Karamazov*; the antiutopian work of Huxley, Zamiatin, and Orwell is unthinkable without "The Legend of the Grand Inquisitor"; it is difficult to envision the complex attitude toward the self in Sylvia Plath's *The Bell Jar* without *The Double* (upon which she wrote a senior honors thesis); and the philosophical parody of Yury Olesha's *Envy* or of Woody Allen's work (either his movies or his early *New Yorker* sketches) could probably not exist without *Notes from Underground*.

Anyone writing about the alienation of modern man from his fellows, anyone writing about philosophically motivated crime, the validation of the self through action, the relation of thought to action, and the justification of criminal means by utopian ends, anyone writing about any of these very contemporary topics cannot ignore the groundwork provided by Dostoevsky in *Crime and Punishment*. It is not so much a matter of the specific influence on specific works; it is an attitude toward the relation between the self and the world that any modern writer imbibes from Dostoevsky. Whether they accept that attitude or reject it, they are partially formed by the experience. Thus, J. D. Salinger, Ernest Hemingway, André Malraux, Jean-Paul Sartre, Albert Camus, Günther Grass, Jerzy Kosinski, John Fowles, Richard Wright, James Baldwin, and a host of others are in Dostoevsky's debt. These names merely begin the list of debtors. Students will come up with many more.

# 3

# Critical Reception

Dostoevsky's work was well received during his lifetime, but his contemporaries never fully grasped the magnitude of his genius. They were confused by the new conception of the life of the mind that he presented, so that a brilliant work like *Notes from Underground* was barely noticed, beyond a vague sense of uneasiness over its nastiness.

*Crime and Punishment* was published serially in Katkov's the *Russian Herald*, simultaneously with Tolstoy's *War and Peace*, as it happens. Reviews were good; the Russian audience, both critical and popular, knew how to recognize and appreciate a good read. The book even earned the tribute of a parody entitled "Malfeasance and Retribution," published in the April 1866 issue of the *Spark*. *Crime and Punishment* touched upon the burning issues of the day and generated the intellectual excitement that readers of the period had come to expect. But few recognized or understood the quantum leap the author had taken over a work like *The Insulted and the Injured* (1862), a hodgepodge of familiar Dostoevskian elements that lacks the cohesiveness and concentration of *Crime and Punishment*.

The year 1866 did mark a turning point in Dostoevsky's career, although the change had more to do with his marriage to Anna

Grigorievna Snitkin than with the publication of any particular work. With his romantic and economic life stabilized (even his compulsive gambling stopped eventually), he was now capable of sustaining long periods of high-quality creativity, and the great novels flowed from his pen with unaccustomed ease. Of the novels published before *Crime and Punishment*, only *Notes from Underground* rises to the level of greatness; of those published after it only *The Eternal Husband* and *A Raw Youth* do not.

His popularity with the reading public had much to do with his visibility in the sociointellectual life of St. Petersburg during the 1870s, and his defense of nationalistic and conservative causes, while it brought him no love from the Left, may have enhanced his overall popularity. For a few decades after his death, Dostoevsky's reputation went into decline. The symbolist movement dominated the turn of the century, sometimes called the Silver Age of Russian culture (contrasted with the Golden Age of the novel, when Dostoevsky and Tolstoy flourished). The early symbolists were interested in poetry and short prose rather than the novel, and their works were characterized by aesthetic concerns rather than the intense intellectuality characteristic of Dostoevsky. As symbolism came to dominate Russian letters during the 1880s, Dostoevsky's popularity faded. But it was not a symbolist but the radical critic Mikhailovsky who voiced most cogently the distaste readers felt for Dostoevsky during these years. In his essay "A Cruel Talent" Mikhailovsky argued that Dostoevsky focuses morbidly on the predatory elements in the human personality. There is no question that the features Mikhailovsky mentions are present in Dostoevsky's work. But it has taken the twentieth century to demonstrate the perspicacity of Dostoevsky's diagnosis of the human condition.

With the turn of the century came a new generation of symbolists, a shift in the concerns of the movement, and a consequent renewal of interest in Dostoevsky. An interest in mysticism led the second generation of symbolists to reevaluate Dostoevsky. This mystical aspect of the symbolist movement had been implicit all along. If symbolism was to be more than a poetic *divertissement*, it needed to present the symbol as something more than a literary device; the symbol had to be a path to transcendent reality. It could only do this by representing the divine in a mystical way, by participating spiritually in the reality it conveyed. The second generation of symbolists returned to the spirit/body dualism of idealistic philosophy that had surrounded Dostoevsky in his youth. The wheel had come full circle.

It was D. S. Merezhkovsky, the mentor of all the young symbolists, who first enunciated both the mystical side of the movement and also the symbolist interest in Dostoevsky. He contrasted Dostoevsky, "the seer of the spirit," with Tolstoy, "the seer of the flesh."

The symbolists found much to like in *Crime and Punishment*. They liked to speak of the ideal of beauty and wisdom, an ideal symbolized by a feminine figure directly related to *hagia Sophia* (holy wisdom) in both Greek and Russian Orthodox theology. Sofia is, of course, the formal name for which Sonya is the nickname, and the symbolist mentality found in Sonya Marmeladova, at once sexual and innocent, redemptive both in her suffering and in her veneration of suffering, an outstanding incarnation of this feminine ideal. Furthermore, when Sonya urges Raskolnikov to kiss the earth as he begins to expiate his crime, she ties herself to the most powerful feminine figure in Russian folklore, dating from pre-Christian times, the barely anthropomorphized fertility goddess, "moist mother earth" (*mat' syra zemlya*). In Sonya, the virgin whore, intersect the most powerful feminine symbols of both Orthodox theology and Russian folklore. Small wonder the symbolists loved her. Vyacheslav Ivanov, both a symbolist poet and a classical scholar, connected these Christian and folkloric themes with Greek mythology and the theory of tragedy. The following quotation gives a good sense of the flavor of Ivanov's Dostoevsky criticism, and that of other symbolists:

> [The] proud son of Earth. . . , aspiring to superhuman power, supposes that the more he alienates himself from the organic, the universal and the primitively real—whose vigour he has hitherto drawn from the all-nourishing mother-soil—the more he will exalt himself. . . . [He] is guilty in the sight of Earth, and receives absolution through his expiation made unto Earth. When he has done this, then she, the patient and silent, who in her universal acceptance has

taken his guilt upon herself, at the end reveals herself . . . and strengthens him.[1]

Other "fertile" ground existed for symbol chasing in *Crime and Punishment*: murder as a symbol for man's guilt, indeed, philosophically motivated murder as symbol of rebellion against God and the earth; murder as initiation rite, not to mention the prevalence of crosses, rivers, and bridges; and the symbol-laden dreams of sleazy old Svidrigailov. The symbolists were also interested in madness and unconventional sexuality, both of which are, at least implicitly, present in Dostoevsky. How ironic that Dostoevsky's first real posthumous following in Russia grew up in this group of prerevolutionary bohemians—but it has ever been Dostoevsky's fate to be adored by groups and individuals he would have abominated.

This interest in Dostoevsky's mystical spirituality was shared by several young theologians during this Silver Age of Russian culture just before the revolution (although most of them focused their attention on *The Brothers Karamazov* rather than *Crime and Punishment*). Vladimir Solovyov, who was both a theologian and a symbolist poet, had been a close friend and protégé of Dostoevsky during the 1870s. Vasilii Rozanov tried a unique route to gaining mystical understanding of Dostoevsky—he married Polina Suslov, the author's fickle girlfriend of the mid-1860s, in an apparent effort to get closer to the master. Suslov had calmed down in middle age and was now ready to capitalize on her early attachment to genius. Jewish theologian Lev Shestov also moved on the fringes of the symbolist movement, and like Merezhkovsky he cast Dostoevsky and Tolstoy as cosmic opposites. But it was Nikolai Berdyaev who most successfully put Dostoevsky's work into theological perspective during this period. Formerly a Marxist (Menshevik), he became a member of the "Landmarks" group that sought to redefine Russia's sense of its own identity in the light of the momentous changes that were obviously impending. Berdyaev devoted an entire book to Dostoevsky; in addition, his theological books are saturated with a mystical nationalism that he abstracted from Dostoevsky's work. Berdyaev saw *Crime and Punishment* as an illustration of the crisis of modern consciousness, "the suicide of man by self-affirmation."

> Dostoevsky studied the results of man's obsession by his own dei-fication under several forms, individual and collective. . . . Every-thing is allowable when it is a question of the unbounded freedom of the superman (extreme individualism), or of the unbounded equality of all (extreme collectivism). . . . Raskolnikov answered the question whether or not he had the right to kill a human being in furtherance of his "idea" solely by reference to his own arbitrary will. But the answering of such a question does not belong to man but to God, who is the unique "higher idea." And he who does not bow before that higher will destroys his neighbour and destroys himself. That is the meaning of *Crime and Punishment*.[2]

Berdyaev came to be called an existentialist once the term was coined, and he led the theistic wing of that movement in France later in the twentieth century, for he taught philosophy at the Sorbonne until his death in 1948.

At the same time the late symbolists and their theologian friends were studying Dostoevsky in Russia the novelist was having his first surge of popularity abroad. To be sure, it was not only Dostoevsky— all sorts of works from exotic Russia were the rage in Western Europe during these years. Turgenev had been the first Russian to be lionized in the West, and it is easy to see why, since he lived in Paris during his last years and was intimate with virtually all the great lights of the French literary scene. A mysterious writer named "Tourghenieff" even shows up in some textbooks of French literature of the period. With the publication in 1886 of *The Russian Novel*, by former French at-taché in St. Petersburg Melchior de Vogüé, Tolstoy and Dostoevsky became known to the Western world. Soon Chekhov and Maksim Gorky were being lionized as well, not to mention Chaikovsky and Musorgsky. And soon Diagilev's Russian ballet was enthralling, and enraging, dance lovers with Nidzhinsky's interpretations of the early Stravinsky ballets. Not only had the eastward flow of cultural influ-ence reversed directions and gone west, the flow had become a deluge.

Constance Garnett's fine English translations popularized Dostoevsky's work in Edwardian England, while Isabel Hapgood's were favored in America.

It is hard to explain Dostoevsky's popularity among the literary bohemians of London's Bloomsbury district during these years. By and large their interest was more psychological and literary than spiritual and religious, although J. Middleton Murry, who stood on the fringe of the Bloomsbury crowd, wrote a book on Dostoevsky that sounds quite like what a Vyacheslav Ivanov or a Lev Shestov was saying:

> [We] must be prepared to discern in [Dostoevsky's characters] . . . clearly symbolic figures. They are real, indeed, and they are human, but their reality and humanity no more belongs to the actual world. . . . They have no physical being.
>
> Ultimately they are the creations not of a man who desired to be, but of a spirit which sought to know. They are the imaginations of a God-tormented mind.[3]

Freud was also a guru for Bloomsbury (it was, after all, Lytton Strachey's brother who translated the standard English edition of the Viennese psychotherapist), and the Bloomsbury group seemed to sense the way in which Freud's view of the mind was prefigured in Dostoevsky. Central to the English appreciation of Dostoevsky were Edward and Constance Garnett, who, if not members of the Bloomsbury set themselves, were the parents of a prominent Bloomsbury artist. It was Constance Garnett who produced the translations of Dostoevsky (and other Russian masters) that remain among the best—when purged of the occasional error or discreet euphemism—for their rendering of the feel of Dostoevsky's Russian into idiomatic English. And literary critic Edward Garnett wrote perceptively on Dostoevsky, although the Slavic writers he was most interested in were Turgenev, Tolstoy, Maksim Gorky, and above all the Anglicized Pole Joseph Conrad. Bloomsbury published Dostoevsky as well. When "Stavrogin's Confession," the suppressed chapter of The Devils, came to light, Leonard and Virginia Woolf published the English translation. And the Woolfs' Hogarth Press published translations of Dostoevsky and others by S. S. Koteliansky, rather oddly giving bylines to people like Woolf, D. H. Lawrence, and Middleton Murry (who knew no Russian) as cotranslators.

But of all the writers associated with Bloomsbury, D. H. Lawrence wrote most interestingly on Dostoevsky. Lawrence claimed to hate Bloomsbury, although he was well acquainted with most of its members. He also claimed to hate Dostoevsky, although he read him with passionate excitement. His appreciation of Dostoevsky has the air of a sweat-soaked fistfight out of *Women in Love*. Two masters with diametrically opposed ideas are engaged in mortal combat. The following is from a letter to Koteliansky:

> Thank you for the little Dostoevsky book. I have only read Murry's Introduction and "Dream of a Queer Fellow." Both stink in my nostrils. Dostoevsky is big & putrid, here, Murry is a small stinker, emitting the same kind of stink. How is it that these foul-living people ooze with such loving words. "Love thy neighbor as thyself"—well & good, if you'll hate thy neighbor as thyself. I can't do with this creed based on self-love, even when the self-love is extended to cover the whole of humanity.—No, when he was preaching, Dostoevsky was a rotten little stinker. In his art he is bound to confess himself lusting in hate & torture. But his "credo"—!—My God what filth.[4]

But he also wrote elsewhere to the same Koteliansky: "[Dostoevsky] is a great man & I have the greatest admiration for him. I even feel a sort of subterranean love for him."[5] Lawrence was offended by Dostoevsky's idea of salvation through self-denial and suffering, and he opposed it with his own idea of phallic self-affirmation. The two were in agreement about the structure of human relationships, but they looked through opposite ends of the telescope. And Lawrence loved *Crime and Punishment*, except for the ending, which in his opinion ruined the whole thing.

Dostoevsky has been particularly important as a background for twentieth-century existentialist thought and literature. The term "existentialism" is vague enough to be applied to figures as disparate as the atheist Jean-Paul Sartre and the Catholic Jacques Maritain; what ties the existentialists together is a primary focus on the passionately believing subject rather than on the ideas that subject embraces. It is easy to see why these thinkers were fascinated by *Crime and Punishment*, in which the believing subject's idea carries him across conventional boundaries into criminality. Dostoevsky is universally acknowledged to be one of the seminal thinkers of the "existentialist movement," along with Danish theologian Søren Kierkegaard and German "nihilist" (the genuine rather than the Russian sort) Friedrich Nietzsche.

The existentialist movement flowered in France, and an interest in Dostoevsky was de rigeur for French existentialists. While the Christian wing of the movement (Maritain, Gabriel Marcel) had a direct conduit to the Russian tradition in the person of Nikolai Berdyaev, it was the atheistic existentialists who became better known for their restatements of the Dostoevskian dilemmas in terms of modern alienation, and for finding answers to the questions different from those Dostoevsky himself had proposed. Only André Gide wrote a full-blown book on Dostoevsky, but the Russian novelist is very present as a background in the work of Camus, Sartre, and André Malraux. Camus says:

> All of Dostoevsky's heroes question themselves as to the meaning of life. In this they are modern: they do not fear ridicule. What distinguishes modern sensibility from classical sensibility is that the latter thrives on moral problems and the former on metaphysical problems. In Dostoevsky's novels the question is propounded with such intensity that it can only invite extreme solutions. Existence is illusory *or* it is eternal. If Dostoevsky were satisfied with this inquiry, he would be a philosopher. But he illustrates the consequences that such intellectual pastimes may have in a man's life, and in this regard he is an artist.[6]

The psychoanalytic community maintained a lively interest in Dostoevsky's work. *Crime and Punishment* has probably inspired more psychoanalytic criticism than any other work of literature, except perhaps *Hamlet* or *Oedipus Rex*. Freud's own work on Dostoevsky is disappointing. He spends most of his energy trying to prove the unsupportable conclusion that the news of Dostoevsky's father's murder caused the onset of his epilepsy, and talking about the link between compulsive gambling and masturbation. The preoccupation with parricide relates more to *The Brothers Karamazov*, where a mysterious murder seems a dramatic confirmation of Oedipal theory. But in fact *Crime and Punishment* provides more fruitful ground for psychoanalytic criticism, with its convoluted motivations for murder and with its glimpse into the unconscious musings of the murderer. A number of interesting studies have been written, both by practicing psychiatrists and by literary specialists, among which the work of G. Roheim, J. Thomas Shaw and A. L. Bem (excluded from the Bibliography, as his work is unavailable in English) are particularly noteworthy. Richard Rosenthal's article, quoted here, is a good example of the best psychoanalytic work on Dostoevsky:

> Psychic murder, the attempt to annihilate painful and unacceptable aspects of the self, underlies the murder of the old pawnbroker and her sister. Raskolnikov believes that frustration and pain can be evaded by destructively attacking the part of the mental apparatus able to perceive them. Thoughts are treated as unwanted things, fit only for expulsion. Such pathological projective identification results in violent fragmentation and the disintegration of the personality; the evacuated particles are experienced as having an independent life threatening him from outside.[7]

After the revolution, Dostoevsky was suppressed in the Soviet Union, as much for the psychosexual perversion that seemed implicit in his work as for his religious mysticism and political conservatism. Freud has always been taboo in the Soviet literary and psychiatric establishment, particularly during the Stalin years, and the very fact that Dostoevsky's work seemed unusually amenable to Freudian criticism made him suspect. The work of Turgenev and Tolstoy has always been more acceptable to the Marxist-Leninist literary establishment, despite their aristocratic backgrounds, both because of their stylistic conservatism and because of the criticism of the tsarist regime implicit and sometimes explicit in their work. Only Dostoevsky's early work, *Poor Folk* and the like, was appreciated, and Dostoevsky was bound in the straitjacket of "critical realism" in which the alienation of a Raskolnikov or an underground man is seen as a critique of the perverted economic structure of his society. Exceptions to this rule have been the fine biographical work of Leonid Grossman and A. S. Dolinin and the writings of G. M. Fridlender (the latter two have been excluded from the Bibliography, as their work is unavailable in English).

The only exception to this bleak picture was the brilliant work done on Dostoevsky by Mikhail Bakhtin, who saw Dostoevsky's uniqueness in terms of dialogical or polyphonic character (see chapter 6). Dostoevsky allows opposing points of view to speak with comparable credibility, engaging each other, and the reader, in genuine dialogue. Despite his brilliance, Bakhtin's ideas on Dostoevsky are extremely difficult to assess. To begin with, dialogical features comprise far more than a set of literary principles for Bakhtin. He is trying to assemble materials for an all-embracing philosophical system and he is using Dostoevsky as a starting point. Furthermore, Bakhtin was suppressed, he altered some of his writings to get them into print, published some of them pseudonymously or with the bylines of friends, and he published writings on other topics in books nominally devoted to Dostoevsky. As a result, Bakhtin's ideas on Dostoevsky are a tangled skein that has only recently begun to be unraveled.

The contemporary work on Dostoevsky is diverse. Interesting work has been done on recurrent imagery (situation rhyme, spatial form) as a structural principle for Dostoevsky.[8] Psychoanalytic critics continue to do interesting work on *Crime and Punishment*.[9] Post-Bakhtinian studies of narrative structure and reader response have dominated the recent scene.[10]

Dostoevsky will continue to be a hot topic in literary studies as long as men and women feel alienated from society and try to validate themselves and their ideas through action, and in fact, as long as they enjoy a good read.

*a reading*

# 4

# Part 1

## Narrative Structure

The first chapter of *Crime and Punishment* plunges us, as readers, into the mind of a man about to commit murder. As critics or analytical readers, we must step back a bit and ask how this happens. In doing so we will learn some important things about the structure of the novel, a structure based on the consciousness of the protagonist.

Raskolnikov's decision to murder the old pawnbroker, and later his indecision about whether or not to confess, remains the skeleton of the novel; it is constantly ticking away like a clock or time bomb buried in Raskolnikov's mind—and in ours. Yet this central event is often submerged by the novel's surface events, which belong to a variety of seemingly unrelated subplots: the tribulations of the Marmeladov family, the romantic misadventures of Dunya Raskolnikov, the sleazy perversions of Svidrigailov. Some of the surface events, however, are not tied to any subplot: Raskolnikov's encounter with a drunken girl in 1:4, his observation of a suicide attempt in 2:6, his ventures into the nightlife of St. Petersburg. But these extraneous events are related to a set of themes of patterns very important to Raskolnikov as he muses about himself, his relationships with others, and the meaning of his criminal experiment.

So, in talking about the structure of *Crime and Punishment*, we may distinguish between main plot events (related to the murder), subplot events (related to Raskolnikov's family and friends), and nonplot events (related only thematically to the others). The structure of the novel is formed not only by the alternation between plot and subplot, but by a thematic structure that ties plot and subplot together and draws nonplot events into the whole.

The structure of the novel is the structure of Raskolnikov's consciousness. As we read, we are immersed in the immediate context of his thoughts, and we are not troubled by structural questions. The novel's structural complexity is implied by Raskolnikov's mind, which ties together his central project, his relationships with family and friends, and the themes that govern his view of the world, including perceptions of extraneous events. It is our immersion in this mentality that produces the novel's complexity and at the same time renders us untroubled by it.

How has Dostoevsky managed to immerse us so completely in Raskolnikov's mind? One would think that this could be done most effectively with a first-person narrator, that is, a central character who is telling his own story. Indeed, Dostoevsky's most penetrating look at the life of the mind prior to *Crime and Punishment* was the short novel *Notes from Underground*, narrated by its protagonist. It appears that this was the novelist's first impulse for *Crime and Punishment* as well, for the earliest drafts available to us from the author's notebooks present Raskolnikov as the teller of his own story.

A passage from "Under Indictment," one of these drafts, may show us why Dostoevsky changed his mind and used a third-person narrator. Here are the opening lines of "Under Indictment": "I am under indictment and I will tell everything. I will write everything down. I am writing for myself, but let others read it. Let all my judges read it if they want to. This is a confession. I will hide nothing." Right away we see the fundamental advantage and the fundamental problem of making the text a first-person memoir. The advantage is that it gains immediacy by coming from the source; the disadvantage is that it loses that very immediacy as it must be imagined as a later

A page from the notebooks for *Crime and Punishment*. (The sketches are unidentified. The heading reads "Plan. After the dream." See Edward Wasiolek, *The Notebooks for 'Crime and Punishment'* [Chicago: University of Chicago Press, 1967] p. 151–53, for translation.)

composition put down on paper long after the fact. Even from the point of view of psychological credibility this is a loss, as the protagonist is sure to have forgotten (or repressed) details of his own emotional state as he has revised his own attitude toward the events in retrospect.

How can the immediacy and credibility of first-person narration be preserved in a narration simultaneous with the events narrated? If we think of the text literally, as a written thing, the premise is too implausible: "I am now raising the axe over my head with both hands." This will never do. With which hand is he holding the pen? Where is the paper? And why on earth is he writing at a time like this?

In fact, to make a first-person narration simultaneous with the events narrated introduces an element of "magic"—we become magically privy to the protagonist's self-conscious utterances, which are not written down, but directed to us as the events unfold. In fact, if a premise so implausible is to be introduced anyway, a third-person voice will actually reduce the reader's sense of the artificiality of this fictional premise. Compare: "I am now raising the axe over my head with both hands" to "He raised the axe over his head with both hands." Both sorts of narration entail a "magical" premise, but the second is less obtrusive, and easier to swallow, than the first. We cease to think of the narration as a written text; we simply suspend disbelief and accept the magic by which the character's thoughts are revealed to us. Earlier fiction never allowed this sort of thing, but its invention made the nineteenth-century psychological novel possible. So the immediacy that might be gained by a firsthand narration is actually better achieved by unobtrusive third-person narration, simultaneous with events.

There is another advantage to a third-person narrator, for Raskolnikov cannot give us a very objective perspective on his own thoughts and activities, and he cannot tell us much about other characters. Dostoevsky's third-person narrator can.

The following passage from "Under Indictment" introduces the first Marmeladov scene (1:2) and displays a disconcerting fuzziness, resulting from the fact that Raskolnikov is presenting, in retrospect, his own acutely disturbed consciousness: "I don't even remember very clearly how it was that I walked up to the bar, took out my tiny silver ring (from some monastery or other—it came to me from my mother) and somehow persuaded them to give me a bottle of beer for it. Then I sat down and as soon as I drank the first glass, my thoughts cleared right away, in a single minute or so. And after that I remember the whole evening, from the moment I drank that first glass, just as though it were imprinted ['coined,' 'minted'] in my memory." The corresponding paragraph in the published novel, too long to quote here, gives a much fuller and clearer account of Marmeladov's psychological state, something Raskolnikov cannot very well do. In terms of immediacy, plausibility, and objectivity, then, a third-person narrator can describe everyone's thoughts and actions more effectively.

But with a third-person narrator, how can the reader be so completely immersed in Raskolnikov's consciousness; how is it that we identify so intensely with his thoughts and feelings? The answer is that, despite the fact that the narrative voice is external, the narrative vantage point is Raskolnikov's. Once we have accepted the "magicality" inherent in the fictional process—that is, once we have stopped trying to make the text plausible as an actual memoir and the narrator plausible as an actual person—all sorts of "magical" combinations are possible. We can distinguish between the "narrative voice" that describes events and the "narrative eye" that observes them. Here, the narrative voice is an objective, external figure, but the narrative eye, the vantage point from which events are observed and thought about, is Raskolnikov's. This puts us as readers right into the thick of the protagonist's anguished quandary, yet it enables us to observe him objectively at the same time. One of the best psychoanalytic critics has pointed out that the narrating figure is very like the perceiving self in a dream, observing without participation the behavior of the acting self.[11]

It was probably in December 1865 that Dostoevsky made the change to third-person narration, while retaining the protagonist's point of view. Here is a passage from the notebooks: "The story is from the person of the author, a sort of unseen, but all-controlling being, but not leaving him for a moment. . . . The story is from my point of view, not his. . . . In some other ways a confession [first-person memoir] would not be the wisest course, and it is difficult to imagine why it would have been written."

The emotional effect upon the reader is extraordinary, for we experience Raskolnikov's emotions as he proceeds toward the murder, even though we understand little about his reasons for wanting to do the deed. The following passage from 1:7 is a good illustration:

> The stairway was narrow, dark and grimy, but he already knew all that, he had checked it out and was pleased with the whole setup. In such darkness, even the most curious gaze would not be dangerous. "If I'm so frightened this time, what would it be like if somehow it should really happen that I were approaching the real thing," he thought involuntarily, going on up to the fourth floor. Here his way was blocked by two retired military porters carrying furniture out of one of the apartments. He already knew in advance that a German family man lived here, a clerk: "It happens that German is moving out now, so, it turns out that, on the fourth floor, on this landing of this staircase, anyway, only the old lady's apartment will be occupied, for a while anyway. That's good . . . just in case. . . ." he thought once again, and rang at the old woman's apartment. The bell tinkled feebly, as though of tin rather than brass. In apartment buildings like this the smaller apartments almost always have such bells. He had forgotten the sound of this bell, and now it was as though its characteristic ring reminded him of something very clearly. . . . He shuddered; his nerves were too weak this time.

Notice how the narrator slips smoothly in and out of Raskolnikov's mind, now quoting his thoughts, now describing them, now giving external descriptions of Raskolnikov and his circumstances. One critic makes a useful distinction between interior monologue ("I just don't care any more"), narrated consciousness ("He just didn't care any more"), and interior analysis ("He knew that he just didn't care any more"). But even in the final version, some of the interior analysis is cast in the form of recollection at a later date ("He later recalled that he just hadn't cared any more").[12] The picture of Raskolnikov's mental life is much fuller and clearer than it could be if it were narrated by Raskolnikov himself, yet it retains the full intensity of Raskolnikov's own stream of consciousness.

That the narrative eye is Raskolnikov's is especially clear in this passage (1:7), where he is looking at the pawnbroker and trying to evaluate her responses to him, immediately before the murder:

> The old woman barely glanced at the "cigarette case," but then immediately fixed her gaze on the eyes of her uninvited guest. She looked at him with attention, suspicion, and malice. About a minute passed. It even seemed to him that there was something resembling mockery in her eyes, just as though she'd guessed the whole thing. He felt that he was losing his resolve, that he was almost frightened, so frightened that it seemed to him that if she had kept on looking at him that way, without saying a word, for half a minute or so, he would have fled from her.

The effect is not only emotional, but ethical as well, for even the most moral reader becomes an accessory to the crime. It is always interesting to query first readers of the novel about their emotional response to the following passages:

> A dark, tormenting thought rose up in him—the thought that he was going crazy and that, even at this very moment, he was unable to make reasonable decisions, unable even to defend himself, and that perhaps he was not doing what needed to be done at all. . . . "My God! I must flee, I must flee!" he muttered, and threw himself into the front hall.
>
> But here awaited him a greater horror than he had ever experienced! He stood and looked, but didn't believe his eyes: the door, the front door, from the foyer onto the stairway, the very same door at which he had just now rung and then entered, stood open, ajar by a whole palm's width, neither the lock nor the sliding bolt was fastened—all the time! The whole time! The old woman had not locked it behind him, perhaps out of caution. But my God! And of course he had seen Lizaveta after that! And how could he, how could he fail to guess that she had of course come in somewhere—

not through the wall! . . .

The steps sounded very distant, still at the very bottom of the stairway, but he remembered very well and clearly that from the very first sound he began to suspect for some reason that they were unquestionably coming *here*, to the fourth floor, to see the old woman. Why? Were these steps so unusual, so portentous or something? The steps were heavy, even, unhurried. Now *he* had passed the first floor; now he had started up the next flight, becoming more and more audible! He could hear the heavy panting of the visitor. Now he's already started the third flight . . . He's coming here! And it suddenly seemed to him as though he had turned to stone; it was exactly as in dreams—they're chasing, they're closing behind, they're intent on murder, but you feel rooted to the spot and cannot even move a finger!

Most readers will admit that they cannot resist hoping that Raskolnikov will escape. This hope may well remain at an unconscious level for most readers, but it may explain the intensity of readers' visceral response to this novel. If some sort of sense of guilt is indeed a universal part of the human experience, then our emotional and ethical identification with Raskolnikov and his crime may well be tied to a basic human drive toward expiation of that guilt. Dostoevsky wants to place us in the position of the guilty Raskolnikov; then as we observe his expiation, it becomes our own.

## OTHER STRUCTURAL QUESTIONS

One further structural question has to do with the way Dostoevsky presents the novel's characters. After finishing the first part, it is a good idea to think back over the characters that have been introduced. A handful of characters have actually appeared and taken part in the action: Raskolnikov himself, the elder Marmeladovs (note that Mrs. Marmeladov is introduced by Marmeladov well before we actually see her), and Alyona Ivanovna and her sister Lizaveta (although the last two have already been murdered by the time part 1 ends). A far more

significant number of characters, in fact almost all of the chief supporting characters, have been introduced by hearsay but have not yet
appeared on the scene. We are introduced to Mrs. Raskolnikov and
her daughter Dunya, through the former's letter. Her letter also tells
us about Svidrigailov and Luzhin. Marmeladov himself tells us about
Sonya. And Razumikhin is described by the narrator, as Raskolnikov
decides to postpone his visit to that friend. (An early draft places this
paragraph in part 2, where Razumikhin appears for the first time, but
in the final version Dostoevsky moved it to 1:4.) This technique of
describing characters by hearsay before they appear is an old theatrical
trick to heighten interest in the character, although it often shows up
in prose fiction as well. (Tolstoy, for example, uses it to good effect in
*Anna Karenina.*) Dostoevsky's reliance on this technique is one of the
reasons his work is often called "dramatic." One could also trace this
technique to the fact that the narrative eye is placed in Raskolnikov's
consciousness. We hear about characters when Raskolnikov thinks
about them; we meet them when he sees them.

It is also worth noting that Dostoevsky relies heavily on "interpolated" or "inserted narratives"—that is, on partially self-contained
subsections (anecdotes, histories, letters, and the like) presented by
characters other than the main narrator. In other novels Dostoevsky
uses interpolated narratives chiefly to reinforce the thematic structures, the themes and behavior patterns of the work as a whole. Here
they are used chiefly to introduce subplots, although since the subplots
themselves reinforce the thematic structure, that goal is not wholly
absent even here. In part 1 of *Crime and Punishment*, chapter 2 is
devoted to a narrative by Marmeladov on the pathetic history of his
family, with particular attention to Sonya's forced recourse to prostitution. Chapter 3 is dominated by Mrs. Raskolnikov's letter, through
which we learn of Dunya's difficulties. Even the dream in chapter 4
may be treated as an interpolated narrative, as it comes from Raskolnikov's unconscious, rather than from his conscious mind where the
novel's narrative eye resides. The conversation overheard in a tavern
at the beginning of chapter 5 is another sort of interpolated narrative
in which an unidentified character plants the idea of the murder in

Raskolnikov's fertile mind. Again, all of these interpolated stories fit into the narrative model suggested above: a third-person narrative voice is recording the events of Raskolnikov's mental life, as perceived by Raskolnikov himself. In part 1 Raskolnikov is encountering a series of "texts" (as the semioticians would say) presented by Marmeladov, Mrs. Raskolnikov, his own dreaming mind, and the unidentified student, and he is responding to them as he decides whether or not to commit the murder (as he "writes" his own "text").

One continuing debate in Dostoevsky studies has to do with the idea that his novels are chaotic, or simply sloppily written. This used to be a truism. In fact, most critics now agree that although the plot structures are often chaotic, and although the novels present a picture of chaotic or frenzied emotional life,[13] the texts themselves are carefully organized around the interplay of basic thematic patterns. It is thematic structure that gives the whole thing its unity. More will be said about this thematic or "abstract" structure later on.

## CHRONOLOGY OF PART 1

| Time | Event/Chapter |
|---|---|
| almost 3 years ago | Raskolnikov leaves home (1:3). |
| 1½ years ago | Marmeladovs move to St. Petersburg (1:2). |
| last year | Dunya goes to the Svidrigailovs (1:3); Raskolnikov's fiancée, the landlady's daughter, dies (2:3). |
| 6 months ago | Raskolnikov leaves school (3:5, 1:3) and writes article on crime (3:5). |
| 4 months ago | Raskolnikov last sees Razumikhin (1:4). |
| 4 months ago | Mrs. Raskolnikov sends money (1:3). |
| more than 2 months ago | Mrs. Raskolnikov's last letter sent (1:3). |
| 2 months ago | Raskolnikov's last letter to mother sent (1:3). |

# Part 1

| 6 weeks ago | Raskolnikov first pawns object with Alyona (1:6); <br> he has idea, hears conversation (1:6); <br> Dunya leaves the Svidrigailovs (1:3); <br> Sonya goes out as prostitute (1:2); <br> Katerina quarrels with landlady (1:2). |
|---|---|
| 5 weeks ago | Marmeladov gets job back (1:2). |
| 1 month ago | Raskolnikov gets "lost in dreams" (1:1, 2); <br> Lebeziatnikov beats Katerina (1:2). |
| 6 days ago | Marmeladov begins binge (1:2). |
| Novel Begins <br> late July P.M. | The "rehearsal" (1:1). |
| the next day | Letter, drunken girl, dream (1:3–5). |
| the next day | The murder (1:6–7). |

The chronology of the remainder of the novel is not so involved. The events of 2:1 take place in one day, which is followed by an indeterminate period of illness, and the rest of parts 2–5 takes place in the next three days. Another indeterminate period begins part 6, but it cannot last more than two or three days, and the remainder takes place in the two days following. The epilogue takes place nine months later.

## GEOGRAPHY

*Crime and Punishment* is closely bound up with the city of St. Petersburg (now Leningrad). The geography of the novel is carefully plotted; it is clear that Dostoevsky had specific buildings and locations in mind. He lived in the Haymarket area, where the novel takes place, while writing it; in fact, his apartment was on Raskolnikov's street, Stolyárny (Carpenters') Lane. Scholars have mapped it all out, in far more detail than is needed for someone who is simply reading the novel, and tourists in Leningrad can even take a very interesting tour of sites associated with this and other novels, ending up at a museum on the other side of town, in an apartment where the Dostoevsky family lived a decade later.

If the novel is so carefully mapped out, how is it that the reader is often confused by its geography? Partly, this is a result of simple unfamiliarity with this particular city, Russian place names, and so forth. But even Russian readers familiar with St. Petersburg/Leningrad are sometimes confused, and this confusion is a result of a specific device beloved by Dostoevsky, which may be termed "situation rhyme." This device is discussed in detail later on, but, put briefly, it is a tendency to present a number of phenomena that are structurally similar, but in fact not quite identical. These may be locations, patterns of behavior, relationships between characters, gestures or movements, even repetitive symbolic patterns. In terms of geography this produces a welter of taverns, houses run by German landladies, bridges, gardens, and the like, and the reader is blinded by their profusion. So a few words on geography are in order.

St. Petersburg/Leningrad is built on the Nevá River delta, so it has many canals, bridges, and embankments (streets running alongside canals). This in itself becomes an important symbolic pattern, as bridges are treated as places of decision, and water becomes associated with the idea of suicide. Three canals run through the central part of town: the Ekaterínsky (Catherine's), the Móika, and the Fontánka. The Ekaterínsky intersects the Haymarket area, where most of the novel's action takes place. The main body of the Nevá divides the city proper from "the islands": Vasílevsky, Peterbúrgsky (Petersburg), Petróvsky (Peter's), and the island fortress of Peter and Paul. The Little Nevá and the Névka are smaller rivers that separate the islands from each other. The bridges mentioned in the novel are the Nikoláevsky (Nikolai's), one of the bridges connecting the city proper with Vasílevsky Island; the Túchkov, connecting that island with the Petróvsky and Peterbúrgsky islands; the Voskresénsky (Resurrection), crossing the Móika just north of the Haymarket; and the Kokúshkin, near Raskolnikov's apartment.

Most of the novel's important characters reside in the Haymarket

St. Petersburg. Haymarket Square.
Lithograph, 1850s.

St. Petersburg. Ekaterinsky Canal.
Artist F. Bagants, 1860s.

area. Raskolnikov lives on Stolyárny Street, just north of Haymarket Square. The pawnbroker and her sister live, and die, in a building on the corner of the Ekaterínsky Embankment and Sadóvy (Garden) Street, just across the Kokúshkin Bridge (some editions incorrectly read "Kámenny [Stone] Bridge"; others say simply "the K—— Bridge").

The Marmeladov family lives quite nearby, although we are not told exactly where, in a building administered by the German landlady Amalia Fyodorovna (or Ludwigovna) Lippewechsel. When Luzhin comes to town, he stays there as well, with his friend Lebeziatnikov.

Readers may confuse Lippewechsel with another German landlady, Luisa Ivanovna, whose German accent provides considerable comic relief in the scene at the police station in 2:1 (as does Lippewechsel's elsewhere). The reputation of Luise Ivanovna's establishment is questionable, and it even seems that Razumikhin visits the place with his friend Zametov (2:3) when he moves to the Haymarket area.

Later on we hear of yet another German landlady, named Resslich, with whom Svidrigailov will lodge. Her reputation is "unquestionable"—she is clearly a procuress. In fact, she could be Darya Franzevna, who first tried to interest Sonya in "the profession" (2:2). She rents a flat to the Kapernaumov family (their name means "Capernaum," the New Testament site of Christ's first miracle, changing water into wine; hence in colloquial Russian "Capernaum" meant "tavern"), who sublet a room to Sonya. The precise location of Sonya's room on the Ekaterínsky Embankment becomes symbolically important later on (see chapter 5). When Dunya and her mother arrive, Luzhin puts them up in Bakaleev's, a disreputable fleabag hotel on Voznesénsky Prospect. The police station and Porfiry Petrovich's office are quite near Haymarket Square.

There is no point listing the profusion of taverns in the novel. It will suffice to say that they are all distinct, and that only one of them is given a name—The Crystal Palace. This establishment actually existed (as did most of the other locations named), but more than that, the name had particular resonance for Dostoevsky. The Crystal Palace in London was the site of the first world's fair in 1851, and it was seen

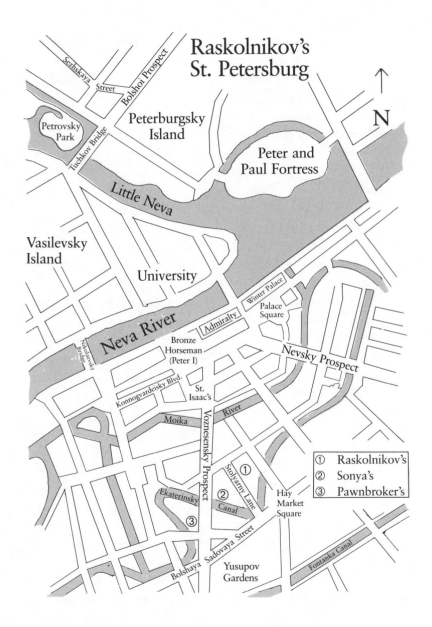

# Raskolnikov's St. Petersburg

N

Sezhskaya Street

Bolshoi Prospect

Petrovsky Park

Tuchkov Bridge

Peterburgsky Island

Peter and Paul Fortress

Little Neva

Vasilevsky Island

University

Neva River

Nikolaevsky Bridge

Winter Palace

Palace Square

Admiralty

Bronze Horseman (Peter I)

Nevsky Prospect

Konnogvardeisky Blvd.

St. Isaac's

Moika River

Voznesensky Prospect

Stolyarny Lane

① 

② 

Hay Market Square

Ekaterinsky Canal

③ 

Fontanka Canal

Bolshaya Sadovaya Street

Yusupov Gardens

| | |
|---|---|
| ① | Raskolnikov's |
| ② | Sonya's |
| ③ | Pawnbroker's |

in Russia and elsewhere as the visible triumph of scientific technology and rationality. Dostoevsky sneers at it in *Notes from Underground* and other writings as a sign of the quantification of human life and a turning away from spiritual values. A tavern named The Crystal Palace is trying to conjure up images of wealth, progress, and modernity, but in the context of the novel it can be seen as a representation of the very values the novel is arguing against.

During his long walk in 1:3–5, Raskolnikov walks along Voznesénsky Prospect toward Vasílevsky Island, encounters the drunken girl on Konnogvardéisky (Cavalry Guards') Boulevard, walks across Vasílevsky Island and toys with the idea of visiting Razumikhin, crosses the Túchkov Bridge and wanders on Peterbúrgsky and Petrovsky islands, finally settling down for a nap in the park on the latter, where he has the dream of the horse. (Svidrigailov's wanderings in part 6 take him to the very same area.) The meditation on freedom in 1:5 takes place on the Túchkov Bridge, and it is easy to see that the trip home via Haymarket Square is indeed a detour.

One final geographical note: Raskolnikov buries the money in 2:2 in a very specific spot on Voznesénsky Prospect. Dostoevsky's wife, Anna Grigorievna, said that the novelist once pointed the spot out to her. Here the geographical scheme of the novel becomes closely tied to its symbolic scheme, for *voznesénsky* means "resurrection," a theme that will become central in the later sections of the novel.

## MOTIVE

The fundamental question of part 1 is "why?" As the section ends, the reader remains just as confused on this question as Raskolnikov is (not surprisingly, as we have seen all the events leading up to the murder through his eyes). The murder is "overdetermined"; there are too many possible answers to the question "why?" Some critics have maintained that the varying motives originated separately in the drafts for the novel, and that the split in Raskolnikov's character is a literary device designed to unify these separate compositional strains.[14]

## Part 1

But beyond this, there are two different kinds of answers to this question. Aristotle would have called them the efficient cause (the series of empirical factors that result in the event) and the final cause (the agent's self-conscious reason or goal in performing the act). Using more contemporary philosophical language, we might call them the positivistic (or scientific) cause and the ethical (or moral) cause. Or, to use language closer to the everyday, we can call them the trigger and the rationale.

Raskolnikov has several related rationales for committing the murder, but, oddly enough, we do not hear much about them until parts 2 and 3, after the murder has been committed. In fact, the article on crime, outlining the theory behind his criminal experiment, is not mentioned until part 3, although Raskolnikov had written it much earlier, and it had been published a few months before the crime. Whether before or after the fact, much of this rationalization seems to be unrelated to the actual trigger.

In any case, Raskolnikov's favorite rationale for the crime may be termed the humanitarian one. This is suggested in 1:6 by the student whose outline of the criminal project Raskolnikov overhears, and appropriates, in a tavern:

> A hundred, a thousand good deeds and projects which might be set in motion and perfected with the old woman's money, now promised to a monastery. Hundreds, perhaps thousands of beings that could be set on the right path; dozens of families saved from poverty, from disintegration, from ruin, from perversion, from venereal disease—and all of this could be done on her money. Kill her and take her money, and with its help devote oneself to the service of all humanity, to the common cause. What do you think? Wouldn't that one tiny little crime be expiated by a thousand good deeds? For one life—a thousand lives saved from corruption and decay. One death and a hundred lives in return—it's simple arithmetic!

It is implied that if Raskolnikov could obtain a large amount of money, he could get his family out of difficulty, continue to help the Marmeladovs, and set himself up in a career benefiting mankind, but all of his actual attempts at charity are confused, bumbling, misdirected, and ineffective.

Of course, central to the humanitarian rationale is the necessity of carrying away substantial money from the old woman's apartment. The artificiality of this rationale becomes increasingly evident as we see that Raskolnikov takes very little booty, and then does not seem to know what to do with it. As he rehearsed his crime, he focused on the moment of the kill rather than the theft, suggesting that we need to look further for an adequate motive.

There is another rationale that comes closer to accounting for Raskolnikov's behavior. Although it is a self-conscious rationale, it brings us closer to the "trigger," that is, to the set of unconscious drives that push Raskolnikov toward his crime. This rationale may be called the existential motive, and it is one of the keys to this novel's uniqueness and brilliance. Raskolnikov is trying to prove something to himself about his own identity (hence the term *existential*—he is trying to make a statement about his existence, about who he is). Of course, part of what he is trying to prove to himself is that he is a benefactor to mankind, and this detail ties the two rationales together. This calls to mind the case of Pierre François Lasener, a French criminal in the 1830s who tried to arouse public sympathy by claiming that he was not a common criminal but had ideological underpinnings for his crime, and was a fighter against social injustice and a victim of society. Dostoevsky wrote on the case in his journal, *Time*, in 1861. (*Time* also published accounts of criminal trials, and saw in them a sort of revelation of type.[15]) The intensity of Raskolnikov's commitment to his idea also suggests the protagonist of Pushkin's Gothic story "The Queen of Spades," perhaps another prototype for Raskolnikov.[16]

The existential rationale is explored more fully in part 3 where the detective Porfiry Petrovich discusses Raskolnikov's article on crime. But there are hints of this motive even in part 1. Raskolnikov wants to establish that he is not merely one of the sheeplike multitudes, who live and die leaving no mark on history, but a person of strength and will who takes events into his own hands and changes their course, overstepping whatever boundaries stand in his way. The hints at this motive are submerged in part 1, and occasionally they are negative: Raskolnikov is horrified from time to time that he could plan such an act. Elsewhere he aspires to the strength to do the deed. Whether expressed positively or negatively, at issue is what sort of person Raskolnikov is. "I want to attempt such a deed, and yet I am afraid of such trifles. . . . A man holds everything in his hands, but he still lets everything pass him by, simply from cowardice. . . . It's interesting . . . what do people fear most? A new departure, a new word, one's very own, that's what they fear most. . . . Can I really be capable of *that*?" (1:1) " 'Oh my God! How repulsive all of this is! And can I really, can I really . . . no, it's nonsense, it's ridiculous,' he added decisively. 'And how could such a horrible thing come into my head? What disgusting things, after all, my heart is capable of. Most of all, how disgusting, base, and vile, vile! . . . And I, for a whole month. . . !' " (1:5).

Given Raskolnikov's youth, it is quite possible to think of the murder as an initiation rite. Even the term used for "punishment" (*nakazánie*) in the title, has the alternate meaning of "instruction" or even "initiation." Such initiation rites or rites of passage are often the stuff of novels (*Tom Jones, David Copperfield, The Red and the Black, Huckleberry Finn*) and films (*Star Wars*, and *Summer of '42*). Making the proof of manhood an experimental murder, Raskolnikov fuses questions of personal identity and ethics in a way that has been a seminal influence on the existentialist thinkers of the twentieth century.

Dostoevsky's contribution to modern psychology consists largely in the insight that behavior is conditioned not so much by rational acts of will as by unconscious, irrational drives. It is these drives that "trigger" the act, but in the process we see Raskolnikov vacillating involuntarily between two opposing clusters of emotions and ideas. On the one hand, when he is leaning toward committing the murder, Raskolnikov feels revulsion toward other people and tends to isolate himself from them. And at these times he feels that his actions are determined. After the murder, concealing the crime will take its place on this side of the ledger. On the other hand, when Raskolnikov is resolved not to kill the pawnbroker, he feels free and wants to associate with people, toward whom he feels compassion. After part 1, confessing to the crime will be linked to these emotions. These networks of emotional states constitute the trigger of the murder as distinguished from its rationale. Revulsion, either against the murder or against humanity, is most often the trigger for Raskolnikov's move to the opposing cluster of feelings, but a sense of fate or determinism, brought on by coincidence, can have the same effect.

In chapter 1, on his way to the "rehearsal" of the murder, Raskolnikov feels revulsion as he observes the drunks staggering out of the reeking taverns. But after the rehearsal, his revulsion is directed against the idea of the murder itself, as noted in the previous quotation. Apparently as a result of this new decision, this turning away from the murder, he feels freed from a burden as he enters a tavern, and he feels sociable: "he looked around cheerfully, as though suddenly freed from some terrible burden, and he cast friendly glances at the people in the tavern." At the end of chapter 2, after hearing Marmeladov's story and accompanying him home, this sociability turns to an act of charity toward the Marmeladovs: he gives them money. But this very act of charity seems to push him in the other direction once again. He feels revulsion against people, and this in turn produces the conclusion that "there are no boundaries," that he will commit the murder: "Well, what a foolish thing I've gone and done! . . . After all, they've got Sonya to help them out, and I need the money myself. . . . Mankind is so vile—it can get used to anything. . . . But if man is not vile, . . . then everything else is—prejudice, . . . and there are no boundaries, and that's the way it should be!" His thoughts are quite confused at this point. He says he feels revulsion, that man is vile, but he concludes that if he is wrong and man is not vile, then there are no boundaries (to the commission of crime, and so he may commit the murder). He invokes the favorite concept of the nihilists, overcoming prejudice in favor of the natural sciences, to justify his project. Even though he bases his project on the optimistic, leftist view that man is good, the whole meditation, and consequently the idea of the murder, proceeds from his revulsion against mankind. The trigger/rationale distinction helps unravel this confusion. The humanitarian rationale is based on the leftist idea that man can be good if only he will behave rationally or scientifically. But despite this rationale, the murder is actually triggered by antisocial impulses, by revulsion against the "vileness" of mankind. In this passage, then, the trigger and the rationale work at cross-purposes.

The opening of chapter 3 hints at this revulsion, as we are told that he withdraws from society, but the letter from his mother produces a powerful effect upon him, and he leaves his flat "craving space." He is outraged that he is to be the beneficiary of Dunya's charitable act. He is capable of giving charity (to the Marmeladovs), but he will not receive it. In anguish, he concludes that he must act decisively or submit to destiny. In his rationale, the murder is a decisive act to overcome destiny, but in terms of the trigger, the murder represents destiny or the denial of freedom, as we learn toward the end of part 1.

Next Raskolnikov has the encounter with the drunken girl on the street, an encounter that produces first compassion and the desire to help (much as he had helped the Marmeladovs); then he is "stung" by revulsion and reverses himself: "Leave them! What's it to you? Drop it! Let him have his fun. . . . Let them eat each other alive—what's it to me?" As chapter 5 opens he resolves to go to Razumikhin after "*that*, when *that* is all finished and everything is different. . . . After *that!*. . . But will *that* really take place? Will it really happen?" Once again revulsion against humanity has left him resolved to commit the murder, but notice that the murder seems to be taking place of its own accord—Raskolnikov is not mentioned in the sentence: "will *that* take place?" He is acting "almost unconsciously, according to some sort of internal compulsion." The dream of the beating of the horse pushes him once again in the opposite direction, and his revulsion is now directed against the thought of committing the murder. He feels free. "My God! . . . Will I really, will I really in actual fact take the axe, start beating her on the head, beat her brains out . . . will I slip in sticky warm blood, break the lock, steal and then tremble, hide myself, all covered with blood . . . with the axe . . . My God! Will it really happen?" The thought of freedom becomes particularly vivid to him as he stands on the Tuchkov Bridge, one of the many bridges that symbolize decision-making in the novel. But this thought in turn is reversed by the overhead conversation, in which he learns of the perfect opportunity to commit the crime. This seems to represent destiny, and he feels once again condemned to commit the murder, not free. "He went to his flat as one condemned to death. He thought about nothing, and indeed he was totally unable to think rationally. But with his whole being he came to feel that he no longer possessed freedom of the mind or will, and that everything had suddenly been conclusively decided." And in this frame of mind he commits the murder. The pendulum will continue to swing in successive changes, but withholding confession will take the place of murder on the antisocial, deterministic side of its swing; confession will take the place of not murdering on the free, sociable side.

It must be admitted that the novel relies very heavily on coincidence and overheard conversation. This has been an occasion for much criticism, but in fact the coincidence here is quite intentional, feeding into Raskolnikov's sense of determinism. The two pivotal overheard conversations are the one in chapter 5, in which Raskolnikov "inherits" the murder project from the unidentified student, and the one in chapter 6, where, because he has whimsically taken an uncharacteristic detour, he learns from Lizaveta that she will be away at seven, giving him the opportunity to commit the crime unobserved. These coincidentally overheard conversations exacerbate Raskolnikov's sense that he is not free, and that is enough to trigger the cluster of emotions that includes the murder project. Readers should look for further examples of coincidence and overheard conversation in subsequent chapters.

This sense of determinism is carried into the murder scene through a whole series of images and grammatical constructions that suggest that Raskolnikov is acting passively, mechanically, without engagement of the will. Passive verbs, or more properly speaking, reflexives with passive meaning, are used to describe his thoughts and exclamations, or at any rate, the thoughts become the subject and the thinker the direct object. The extent of this grammatical situation does not really come through in translation, but a literal translation, quite awkward in English, shows what is going on: "At this point the hat recalled itself to him"; "A curse tore itself from his soul"; "When it happened to him that he imagined all of this"; "Here a thought began to interest him"; "this minute stamped itself on him forever"; and even the untranslatable "it thought itself to him" (*emú dúmalos*). (At one point he momentarily, and uncharacteristically, regains the initiative: "this thought flashed in his mind; . . . he himself expelled this thought immediately"—it is the thought about criminals being led to execution.) All of these passages, and other similar ones, are from the last few pages of 1:6, as he proceeds to the murder site. The murder scene itself is peppered with words like "mechanically" and "against his will," culminating with this passage at the very moment of the murder: "It was as though he had no strength at all. But as soon as he had brought down the axe his strength was renewed" ("born"; more on this later).

Irony of ironies! Raskolnikov is committing murder to show that he is the kind of man who can take destiny into his own hands and control it through the force of his will. And the very murder becomes an illustration that he is not free but in the clutches of blind destiny, or perhaps merely of mechanistic cause and effect. This is the first in a series of ironic reversals that Raskolnikov will experience as he explores his punishment-instruction.

# 5

# Part 2

## RUSSIAN NIHILISM

One cannot go far in understanding *Crime and Punishment* without coming to grips with what is termed "Russian nihilism," the version of left-wing ideology that was popular among Russian youth of the intelligentsia during the 1860s. As I explained earlier, Russian nihilism should not be confused with the nihilism ("nothingism," from the latin *nihil*, "nothing") associated with the later existentialist movement, developed by thinkers such as Nietzsche who were indebted to Dostoevsky in significant ways. The Russian nihilists, whom Dostoevsky opposed, were actually utilitarians, stimulated by the work of Jeremy Bentham, John Stuart Mill, and other positivistic philosophers; they were optimistic liberals who believed that a rational utopian society could be constructed based on the principle of the greatest good for the greatest number. The term *nihilist* was applied pejoratively at first, by their opponents, but the radical youth accepted it as it seemed to characterize accurately their vigorous rejection of everything in the old system. These nihilists had great respect for science and believed that ethics must be based on positivistic, materialist, or scientific principles rather than on religious ones. Medicine was a popular field of study among them (although some had received their early training in pre-

seminary grammar schools), and they liked to apply medical meta-
phors to society, seeing it as a diseased organism in need of a cure.
They came not only from the ranks of priests' families but from various segments of Russian society (they were sometimes called *raznochintsy*, "people of various ranks"), reflecting the diversification and
democratization of the intelligentsia that was an important sociological phenomenon of the period. They liked to talk about "the laws of
[human] nature," overcoming "prejudices," and "[enlightened] self-
interest" (or "advantage" or "benefit") as a scientific principle upon
which a utopian society could be constructed. The careful reader will
have recognized in this list terms already encountered in the early parts
of *Crime and Punishment*.

But the nihilism of this novel is not a straightforward presentation
of the typical features of the movement. (For this we have Turgenev's
*Fathers and Sons*, whose controversial hero, Bazarov, is by common
consent the quintessential Russian nihilist of the 1860s.) The only typical nihilist we meet in *Crime and Punishment* is Lebeziatnikov, who
does not appear until part 5 (although we hear of him as early as 1:2),
and who is a ridiculous, if good-hearted, figure. Most of the nihilists
in *Crime and Punishment* come at the movement from some oblique
angle: they have been nihilists in the past but are dismayed by the
movement's naïveté and thick-headedness (not far from Dostoevsky's
own position in *Notes from Underground*), or they are mouthing its
catch phrases for their own purposes. In fact, Dostoevsky's characters
often embody a contradiction between ideology and social type, and
this is nowhere more evident than in the nihilists of *Crime and
Punishment*.

Is Raskolnikov's murder a nihilist one, and is the novel, then, a
straightforward attack on the nihilist movement? Most of Raskolnikov's intellectual rationalization of the murder comes after the fact
and stays away from explicit nihilism. It is not the surface features of
nihilism that are being attacked here, but the positivistic basis of its
system of ethics—that is, the fact that it permits no ethical absolutes
except a commitment to scientific rationality and the ever-shifting
good of society, with the possible corollary that ends may justify

means. This attack on the basis rather than the specifics of Russian nihilism raises the novel out of its place and time and enhances its universality. But it can also produce some confusion.

In fact, the young nihilists of *Crime and Punishment* are all *ex*-nihilists. We assume that they are nihilists because every detail about them as social types suggests this. They are ex-students, eking out an existence in the capital by translating, tutoring, and writing pieces for the liberal press. One of them (Zosimov) has just completed medical school. A number of their names sound religious, suggesting a family background in the clergy and an education in a pre-seminary grammar school. In the social history of the Russian Left this was the background of Vissarion Belinsky, Nikolai Dobrolyubov (whose name means "lover of the good"), and Joseph Dzhugashvili (Stalin). In *Crime and Punishment* it is suggested by the names Zosimov (after Saint Zosima; Dostoevsky later used the name for his hero of faith in *The Brothers Karamazov*), Kheruvimov (Cherubim), Razumikhin (from *rázum*, "wisdom," "good sense"; in reality the name ties his ancestral background to the clergy; symbolically it suggests that he bears qualities of wisdom and good sense in the novel), and Raskolnikov himself (from *raskól*, "schism," "split"; in reality the name ties his family background to the "schismatic" Old Believer sect; symbolically it suggests a neurotically divided character or a split with reality).

The tension between nihilist social type and antinihilistic or ex-nihilist opinion is clearest with Razumikhin. The reader hears about him in part 1, chapter 4, and, if he or she is a Russian reader in 1866, is immediately reminded of Rakhmetov, the nihilist hero of Chernyshevsky's pronihilist novel *What Is to Be Done?* In the notebooks for *Crime and Punishment*, Razumikhin is occasionally even called Rakhmetov. It is particularly the references to Razumikhin's extraordinary physical stamina that remind us of Rakhmetov.

[Razumikhin's] external appearance was striking—he was tall, thin, always poorly shaved, black-haired. Occasionally he would get into a brawl, and he was known for his great strength. One night, carousing with friends, he laid out with a single blow a certain officer of the law who was well over six feet tall. He could drink endlessly, or just as easily abstain. He could be an outrageous practical joker, but could refrain from that as well. Razumikhin was also remarkable in that bad fortune never upset him and it seemed that no unpleasant circumstances could keep him down. He could lodge on a roof if necessary, tolerate terrible hunger or extraordinary cold. He was awfully poor, but insisted on supporting himself, coming by money with whatever jobs he could find. He knew a multitude of sources of income. Once he went a whole winter without heating his apartment, and he insisted that he liked that even better, since one sleeps better when chilly. Currently he had been obliged to discontinue his university studies [a draft states explicitly that he had been expelled, with the clear implication that it was for radical activities], but not for long, and he was exerting all his efforts to arrange things so that he could continue as soon as possible. (1:4)

Compare this with Chernyshevsky's Rakhmetov:

Rakhmetov was at this time twenty-two; he had been a student since the age of sixteen, but had left the university for almost three years. . . . Everyone who knew him, knew him by [the] nickname . . . "the rigorist." At 16½ it occurred to him that he should develop his physical resources, and he began to work on himself. He began a serious program of gymnastic exercises. . . . He began to work as a physical laborer at jobs requiring exceptional strength; he went through many jobs and changed them often, since from every new job, with every change, he would develop a different muscle group. He took up a boxer's diet: he nourished himself . . . exclusively with things that had a reputation for enhancing physical strength, primarily beef, practically raw. He continued to live in this manner from that time on. . . . [H]e took up the most severe manner of living. . . . He would not waste a kopek on food other than red meat. . . . With his own money he would buy nothing of the sort: "I haven't the right to spend money on whims I can do without." . . . He dressed quite modestly, although he loved fine things. And in everything else he lived a Spartan life: for instance, . . . he slept on a felt pad, not even permitting himself to fold it double. . . . Gymnastics, physically demanding work, reading: these were Rakhmetov's occupations, always observing the same rule that he observed in his readings, never to waste time on what was not essential.[17]

But Razumikhin's every statement exposes him as a former nihilist. His account of his relations with the pamphlet publisher Kheruvimov shows that although he is willing to make his living translating and ghost writing for the liberal press, he is contemptuous of their facile posturing, naive phrase mongering and slavish adoration of everything Western European.

> Look, I've got no pupils right now, but hell with them, there's this bookseller Kheruvimov in the Rag Market, and he's just as good as giving lessons. I wouldn't trade him for tutoring jobs with five wealthy merchants. He puts out these editions of trashy booklets on the natural sciences—and do they ever sell! The titles alone are priceless. You've always said I was stupid. Well, by God, here's somebody even dumber than me! Now he's crawled into the movement, although he doesn't understand a thing about it. But I encourage him, of course. Here's two and a half sheets of German text—the stupidist charlatanism in my opinion. Briefly, it examines the question, "Is woman a human being or not?" And of course it concludes triumphantly that she is. Kheruvimov is planning to issue it in his "Woman Question Department," and I'm translating it. . . . We'll finish this and then start translating something about whales, and a bit of the second part of Rousseau's *Confessions*, some dreary gossip he's marked out—we'll translate it. Someone told him that Rousseau is a sort of Radishchev [a major literary figure in the Russian radical left during the late eighteenth century]. I don't contradict him of course. To the devil with him! So, do you want to translate the second part of "Is Woman a Human Being?" (2:2)

In defense of his relations with the bribe-taking police clerk Zametov, Razumikhin excoriates the knee-jerk leftist Zosimov for writing off certain useful people because of their supposedly retrograde habits: "Principles! You're so obsessed by your principles, just as though you were on springs—you can't even turn around of your own volition. In my opinion, he's a good man. . . . So what if he takes bribes! . . . He needs to be won over, not pushed away. You won't improve a man by pushing him away, all the more so if he's just a kid, like Zametov. . . . You thick-headed progressives! You don't understand anything" [2:4]. In 3:5 Razumikhin attacks the Left for its emphasis on extenuating environmental circumstances in the prosecution of crime, and its consequent devaluation of the individual's personal moral responsibility (this was to become an increasingly important hobbyhorse for Dostoevsky in his own writings on Russian domestic affairs in the 1870s). Some of Razumikhin's statements sound quite like something from the more conservative Slavophile camp: "For almost two hundred years we've lost the knack for attending to practical matters!" he remarks to Luzhin, countering Luzhin's comment about the practicality of the "movement." He could only mean, "since the reforms of Peter the Great (1689–1725)." But that would be an antinihilist, Slavophile position.

It is Luzhin, after all, who enunciates most clearly the doctrines put forward by the nihilists. But, once again, there is no match between ideology and social type, for Luzhin is the opposite of a young radical—he is a self-serving, greedy lickspittle, ready to toady, to connive, to mouth fashionable ideas, to take advantage of those in straitened circumstances, and, we finally learn, to frame an innocent person, in order to make his way in the world. His advocacy of utilitarian ethics argues against them more effectively than would any polemic, and he puts the young friends in an absolute rage. The "nihilistic" principle that he outlines is that of "enlightened self-interest" as the law of human nature that governs behavior in society.

> For example, if someone said to me in the past, "Love thy neighbor!" and I did so, what was the result? . . . What happened was that I would tear my kaftan in half and share it with my neighbor, and both of us would remain half naked, just as in the old Russian proverb: "Chase several hares at the same time and you won't catch any." But how science tells us: Love yourself first of all, for all that happens in the world is based on self-interest. If you love yourself alone, then you will manage all your affairs sensibly and your kaftan will remain whole. The truths of scientific economics add that, the greater number of well-organized private affairs in society, the

more, so to speak, whole kaftans, the firmer will be its foundations, and the better organized will be all that pertains to the common good. So it happens that, acquiring things solely and exclusively for myself, it is as though I am, by doing so, acquiring for everyone, and leading to a state of affairs in which my neighbor will get something more than a torn kaftan, and indeed, not from private, individual acts of charity but as a result of the general prosperity. (2:5)

The nihilists argued that an understanding of this "scientific" principle, and of the equivalence of individual interests and the common good, would lay the groundwork for a rational utopia. (American students may be surprised and baffled to recognize an argument we have seen characterized as "trickle down," which is supposedly a conservative rather than a liberal policy. This will not confuse us if we remember that what Luzhin is spouting is a fundamental premise of free-market economics or "liberalism." We tend to identify liberalism as a social conscience toward the poor, but this has only sporadically been a part of liberalism as an economic theory. In this classic sense, liberalism encompasses most of the spectrum of American politics from the far right to the moderate left.) A contemporary reader could not have missed the fundamental strangeness of part 2: a social-climbing, middle-aged lawyer advocating nihilist theory and a group of unshaven, disheveled students opposing it.

The radical Left, in advocating utilitarian economic theory and ethics, assumes that the interests of society and the common good are the ultimate goals; it assumes that the individual will make society's interest his own. Luzhin has done the opposite: he has made his own interest the goal of all. And what makes this abundantly clear is his treatment of Dunya. He wishes to choose a bride who has been disgraced and impoverished, as her condition will enhance her feeling toward him as benefactor and rescuer, which will ultimately lay a foundation for good family relations. As Mrs. Raskolnikov relates, "[H]e decided to take as a bride a girl who was honest but had no dowry, and particularly wanted to take a girl who had experienced an impoverished situation, since, as he explained, a husband should never feel obliged to his wife, and it is much better if the wife considers her husband her benefactor" (1:3). Raskolnikov is a little less polite about this theory: "[I]s it true that you said to your bride . . . that what made you happiest of all was that . . . she was poor . . . since it is more advantageous to take a wife out of poverty, so that you can exercise power over her later, and reproach her with the fact that she has been the beneficiary of your charity?" (2:5). If we view the family as a society in miniature, we then can see Luzhin's perversion of nihilist ethics more clearly: he has treated his own interest, the enhancement of his own position in the family, as the goal, as the common good of the whole family.

Raskolnikov's rage against Luzhin stems first of all from the fact that Luzhin has insulted his sister. But his feelings are more complex than that. We have already noticed that Raskolnikov relishes the role of benefactor, but recoils from that of beneficiary. We have seen that Dunya has made him a beneficiary by marrying Luzhin to save the family (the reverse of Luzhin's treatment of family—the common good really does come first for Dunya), and that Raskolnikov's recoil against the beneficiary role pushed him closer to committing the murder. This unwillingness to accept charity is echoed in part 2 by one of the nonplot incidents that form the thematic structure—when Raskolnikov is given alms because he looks so ragged and has been accidentally hit by the stray lash of a coachman's whip (2:2). In Luzhin, Raskolnikov faces a man who, like himself, enjoys the role of benefactor and who, in fact, has made Raskolnikov's own sister, and indirectly Raskolnikov, the beneficiaries of his charitable ministrations, but who has done so with base, self-serving motives. Small wonder that Luzhin drives Raskolnikov into a frenzy; there are complex personal and ideological reasons for his negative reaction. The relationship between benefactor and beneficiary, between rescuer and rescued, is a fundamental paradigm in this novel.

There is yet another dimension to Raskolnikov's revulsion toward Luzhin, one that relates directly to the murder Raskolnikov has committed. At the conclusion of Luzhin's disquisition on utilitarian economic ethics, Raskolnikov says to him: "Carry to its conclusions what you were just preaching and it follows that people may cut each other's throats!" (2:5). It is not immediately clear why this idea follows from Luzhin's principles. The idea that legal or moral boundaries could be overstepped for the cause, or even that ends justify means, was not a nihilist tenet, as such. Some of the middle premises of this syllogism are hidden, and thus need to be made evident. What utilitarian ethics does that ultimately makes murder permissible is to remove all ethical absolutes except for the common good and to make ethics a mechanistic and scientific, rather than a religious, system. It is in this sense that liberal economic theory implies, for Dostoevsky, that ends justify means, and that crime is permissible for the common good. This will become clearer as we look at Raskolnikov's article on crime in part 3.

Psychologically, what is interesting about Raskolnikov's statement, "If you carry what you were preaching to its logical conclusion, it follows that one may cut people's throats," is that he has found a veiled similarity between himself and the hated Luzhin, in terms of the ideological rationale for the murder he has just committed. Raskolnikov has left nihilism behind, yet gone ahead with the murder, originally planned with a utilitarian-based motive. He has repressed the motive, but gone ahead with the act, because he needs the act for another reason, a truer motive—the existential. In attacking Luzhin, Raskolnikov is attacking himself. Or viewed conversely, Raskolnikov is shifting the blame for the murder he has committed to Luzhin and his theory, one he once shared. These opposite meanings of the accusation can coexist in the world of the novel because they can coexist in Raskolnikov's unconscious mind. This kind of tension between opposite meanings is characteristic of Dostoevsky's writing; it is one of the things that makes his novels vibrate with the intensity of contradiction.

## TWO RECURRENT IMAGES

There is nothing unique to Dostoevsky about using the crossing of a bridge or a river as a symbol for the decision-making process. Language itself, never mind literature, is full of examples of the image:

## Part 2

"Crossing the Rubicon," "Crossing your bridges before you come to them," "Burning your bridges behind you." But St. Petersburg/Leningrad, built on a river delta, is full of bridges, so it is natural that a novel intimately bound up with the life of that city will rely on the "decision on a bridge" paradigm as a special part of the symbolic system. Raskolnikov is constantly swinging back and forth between the extremes of the aggression/submission (murder/no murder, no confession/confession) polarity, and very often the shift occurs while he is on a bridge. In 1:4–5 he takes a long walk, crosses several bridges, has the dream of the horse beating on Petróvsky Island, and returns home via the Túchkov Bridge (near Razumikhin's old apartment) where the following reversal takes place.

> [He] walked onto the Túchkov Bridge. He was pale, his eyes burned, exhaustion filled all his limbs, but he suddenly began to breathe a bit more easily. He felt that he had thrown from his shoulders a horrible burden, which had been oppressing him for a long time, and his spirit suddenly felt lighter and more peaceful. "My Lord!," he prayed, "show me my path, and I renounce that accursed . . . dream of mine."
>   Walking across the bridge, he quietly and peacefully looked at the Neva River, at the bright red sunset. . . . It was as though a boil on his heart, which had been swelling for a whole month, had suddenly burst. Freedom, freedom! He was free now from these spells, from this sorcery, witchcraft, from his obsession. (1:5)

Walking on home through the Haymarket (a detour) he overhears Lizaveta informing him of the perfect opportunity to commit the crime, and the reversal "is reversed."

In 2:5 he goes out for another walk, resolved to make an end of it some way or other. First he finds Zametov in the tavern called The Crystal Palace and mystifies him completely with his cryptic half-confession, then bumps into Razumikhin on the way out of the tavern. His next stop is the Voznesénsky (Resurrection) Bridge. "[He] stopped at the railing in the middle, rested his elbows on it and began to look into the distance. . . . Leaning over the water, he looked mechanically at the last pink reflection of the sunset, on a row of houses, growing dark in the thickening dusk, at one distant window, on a mansard on the left embankment, gleaming, just as though in flames, from the last ray of the sun, which was striking it for a moment." A careful calculation, on the basis of the text of the novel and the map of the city, shows convincingly that this is Sonya's window.[18] His reverie is interrupted by the suicide attempt of an alcoholic floozy named Afrosinya. As he observes this scene, he pulls back from the idea of suicide: "No, it's disgusting . . . water . . . it's not worth it." He is still motivated by the urge to bring things to some kind of conclusion ("All the same, I'll end it, because I wish to") but he will remain alive ("I'll still have my square yard of space"). He will end it by confessing, and he briefly half-looks for the police office, then incriminates himself in front of the workmen at the "scene of the crime." Only his discovery of the dying Marmeladov finally distracts him from his drive to "end it" (that is, kill himself or confess). In any case, his experience on the bridge does pull him back from the suicide option.

If bridges can represent a decision about whether or not to commit suicide, water certainly comes to represent the suicide option, as this Afrosinya episode makes clear. Kulidzhanov's excellent film of the novel depicts one fantasy in which Raskolnikov throws himself from a bridge; although the fantasy never occurs in the novel in precisely that form, the idea is certainly an active one in the system of images that comprise Raskolnikov's mental life. Watch for both of these linkages (bridge/decision, water/suicide) as part 6 progresses.

# 6

# Part 3

## Social Type versus Idea and Personality

In the last chapter I noted that *Crime and Punishment* is populated by a group of bohemian intellectuals who oppose left-wing economic theories, and that they are opposed by an establishment lawyer who upholds those theories. In Luzhin, and in Raskolnikov and his friends, there is a mismatch between social type and ideology. Characters emerge as representatives of clearly defined social groups, but when they open their mouths and begin spouting ideology, as Dostoevsky's characters always do, they do not say the things we expect them to say. Quite the contrary.

This, however, doesn't seem to detract from Dostoevsky's realism. The test of literary realism ought to be the readers' response to the characters as real people, and most readers find in Dostoevsky's characters a humanity so genuine, so vital as to be downright troubling. Not all novelists work this way. Turgenev provides an interesting contrast to Dostoevsky in this regard. They were exact contemporaries, and even acquaintances (though never really friends), but their novelistic techniques are quite opposite. Turgenev deals in types, and he makes them live. Bazarov, the main character of *Fathers and Sons*, has already been mentioned as the quintessential nihilist, a character so typical of his social movement that cultural historians, even today, speak of him as though he had been a real person. Other characters in *Fathers and Sons* share the same kind of typicality: the aristocratic liberal of the previous generation (the "man of the 40s"), the enlightened but not very modern landowner, the old-fashioned country wife. It is their typicality that makes these characters live. After reading about them one feels one knows them because one knows the class they typify.

If Dostoevsky were to create such types, the result would be totally unbelievable cardboard figures, going awkwardly through their predictable paces as they bring a stock novel to its foregone conclusion. In fact, Dostoevsky does occasionally give us such characters—Marmeladov, for instance. Marmeladov is a pathetic drunk; everything in his character harmonizes with this central feature. And although Marmeladov is effective as a minor, stereotypical character, with whom the more interesting characters can react, he borders on the bathetic. If Dostoevsky had created only Marmeladovs, he would not be a great novelist.

For Dostoevsky, as one critic has noted, being true to type is not just a matter of realistic observation of speech details and mannerisms. This would result in mere copying, in a generalization so unindividualized that it must be unreal, since no particular representative of the class would speak that way. Types for Dostoevsky are ideals, in the Hegelian or neo-Platonic sense; they operate vertically. Type-making must have a central and unifying idea or focus for Dostoevsky.[19]

By contrast with the likes of Turgenev, Dostoevsky gives us a type and then knocks it, quite intentionally, askew with a jarring detail that does not fit, a tension between elements of the character that gives it individuality and vividness, that makes it shimmer like one of those graphics in which two images of a word are printed, a micromeasurement apart, so that it seems to vibrate.

The tension is not always between ideology and social type. It may be between personality and social type, as with Katerina Ivanovna Marmeladov, a lover of justice and high society who finds herself trapped in a slum with an alcoholic husband and a terminal disease. And what about Porfiry Petrovich, the fussy, effeminate and scatterbrained police detective (possibly the prototype for Agatha Christie's Hercule Poirot and television's Columbo)?

In fact, we can look at Dostoevskian character as a triangular structure, its three sides formed by personality, social type, and ideology. In all of the interesting, major characters, two of these elements will be in conflict. In Sonya, the meek personality and self-sacrificing Christian ideology are perfectly consonant, but both are jarringly out of tune with their occupation: she is a whore. And she isn't even the typical "whore with a heart of gold," a happy floozy who gives herself merrily to the highest bidder. No, Sonya is a pious, Bible-reading whore. Nowhere but in a Dostoevsky novel would readers buy this. Even there it's difficult.

Then there is Svidrigailov. By the time of his appearance at the very end of part 3, we have heard a good deal about his social type, the sleazy philanderer. As we observe the dialogue between him and Raskolnikov in 4:1, we find that his personality and social type are in harmony. It is his ideas on the supernatural that provide the dissonant element, for he is a spiritualist. Of course he himself is trying to shock Raskolnikov; here it is as though the character, not the author, is intentionally producing the tension between personality/social type (carnal) and ideology (spiritual, in a perverted sort of way).

The issue of types in Russian literature was not a new one in the 1860s. In fact, a preoccupation with social types in literature is a special characteristic of the Russian tradition, distinguishing it from other world literatures. The reason for this, if I may be permitted to generalize, is that Russians look to literature for an expression, an analysis, even a justification, of themselves as a national group, and for argumentation on questions of social, political, and economic organization. By creating a series of characters typifying various elements of society, and by manipulating them through a series of fictional events, one can make a statement about who Russians are, who they ought to be, who are the good/bad guys, where is the polity going, and where it ought to be going. Imagine another literary tradition in which novels have titles like *Who is to Blame?*, *What Is to Be Done?*, *Nowhere to Go!*, *Family Happiness*, *Crime and Punishment*, and *War and Peace*. The poor to mediocre writers of the Golden Age of Russian prose fiction (roughly 1850–1880) had no effective way of dealing with the weight that this tradition added to their literature, and so they wrote drivel like Chernyshevsky's *What Is to Be Done?* in which a troop of ideologically perfect stick figures fights for truth and justice under the very manipulative guidance of an irritatingly self-conscious narrator. Even the good writers of the period, such as Goncharov, Leskov, Saltykov-Shchedrin, and Pisemsky, rose above the problem only occasionally, and they did so in Turgenev's manner, creating types that are so vivid they seem individual. Only the three truly great writers of the period really knew how to handle this problem of type, and each handled it in a completely different way. Tolstoy handled it by ignoring it. Even when he is writing with a distinctly didactic or instructional purpose, he does so with a cast of characters who are total individuals. Turgenev, as already noted, handles it by creating a cast of characters who are at once typical, yet individual. Dostoevsky's solution is perhaps the most unique of the three: he creates a portrait that fits squarely into a social type, then skews it by adding details of personality or ideology that seem to undermine the typicality, making the character vibrantly individual, not to say downright odd.

It was Belinsky, one of Dostoevsky's early mentors, who shaped this tradition of typological characterization. The greatest prose writers of Belinsky's period were Gogol and Pushkin, and each can be seen as a great creator of types. Gogol creates a cartoon gallery of risible caricatures, and to this day Russians use the names of Gogol's characters as a shorthand for identifying personality stereotypes. If someone is a miser call him Plyushkin; a lying braggart is a Nozdryov; a sugary sentimentalist is a Manilov. Gogol had no particular ideological motives for doing this, although he later decided he should, when he came to feel that he should take his mission as a writer more seriously, and so he supplied ideological meanings retroactively. The problem came when he decided to interpret his works as right-wing tracts (most of his friends were Slavophiles), while Belinsky, who adored Gogol's work, had been interpreting him all along as a left-leaning advocate of reform.

Pushkin's work does not fit so clearly into the typological category. Perhaps that is why the interpretations that lay bare the types submerged in his work have been so interesting. Indeed, one critic has argued convincingly that Pushkin's story "The Queen of Spades" creates a plot outline, and a set of character types, that Dostoevsky used as a basis for *Crime and Punishment*, adding the psychological depth and complexity that is so peculiar to Dostoevsky, and not particularly characteristic of Pushkin.[20] But it was Pushkin's contemporary Belinsky who first argued that Pushkin was a creator of types. In a series of articles on *Eugene Onegin* Belinsky argues that the protagonist, whose name the work bears, and the heroine, Tatiana Larin, represent the quintessential types of Russian manhood and womanhood, and in the case of Eugene, it is clearly implied that this is a pathological type, resulting from the perverted social and political system of the nation. In Belinsky's articles on *Eugene Onegin* we have the first formulation of the two ideas that were to become the twin cornerstones of the dominant tradition of Russian literary criticism: the idea that literature should be engagé (politically committed) with a leftist tendency, and the idea that literary argumentation should proceed through the treatment of a series of typological characters.

Oh, yes, there was one other writer, young, liberal, typological, that Belinsky wrote about: Fyodor Dostoevsky with his first novel, *Poor Folk*. The pathetic protagnoist, Makar Devushkin, is a direct imitation of the main character in Gogol's "The Overcoat" and is very like Dostoevsky's later creation, Marmeladov. Belinsky thought the book was wonderful, and he made Dostoevsky famous overnight. The fact that this sort of writing survives into *Crime and Punishment* (indeed, the earliest outlines for the novel call it "The Drunkards" and make the Marmeladov plot central) shows that Dostoevsky was right in his oft-quoted quip: "We all came out from under Gogol's 'Overcoat'!" Belinsky's too.

It was the nihilists, however, who really took the ball from Belinsky and ran with it. They believed with him that the primary forum for sociopolitical argumentation should be literature. To some extent this was a purely practical response to government censorship; one could not come right out and write a straightforward article opposing government policy—that could result in the censor's rejection of the article, the closing of the journal, exile, imprisonment, and perhaps even execution (as Dostoevsky had learned in 1849). It was much safer, and ultimately more effective, to imply one's opposition through literature. In novels, like Chernyshevsky's *What Is to Be Done?*, and in a whole host of journal articles about literature, the nihilists argued their case for reform. The titles of their articles make clear their conviction that literature presents a series of types illustrating the ills of society, ills that they, as scientifically minded "physicians," are prepared to cure: "What Is Oblomovitis?" (a response to Goncharov's *Oblomov*), "When Will the Real Day Come?" (a response to Turgenev's *On the Eve*, which in itself implies a sociopolitical argument— on the eve of what? of reform and emancipation of the serfs?), "The Russian at the Rendez-vous." These nihilists were the intellectual offspring of Belinsky, in turn the intellectual parents of the Bolsheviks and the grandparents of socialist realism. Their tradition has become canonized.

So Dostoevsky is writing within a clearly defined tradition when he creates types. The dissonance he introduces into those types is his signature as a novelist, or one of them anyway. This dissonance has much to do with another "specialty" of Dostoevsky, which we call *polyphony*.

## POLYPHONY

One of the most widely publicized critical theories about Dostoevsky is Mikhail Bakhtin's theory of the polyphonic novel. The very existence of this theory is a good index of the degree to which Dostoevsky's characters break free of the boundaries of type. Briefly stated, Bakhtin argues that Dostoevsky created a new literary genre, the "many-voiced" or polyphonic novel in which we have, instead of an authorial viewpoint imposed from above, a collection of fully valued, independent voices engaging in open-ended dialogue with each other and with the author.

Here is Bakhtin's own statement of the idea:

> The plurality of independent and unmerged voices and consciousnesses and the genuine polyphony of fully valued voices are in fact characteristics of Dostoevsky's novels. It is not a multitude of characters and fates within a unified objective world, illuminated by the author's unified consciousness that unfolds in his works, but precisely the plurality of equal consciousnesses and their worlds, which are combined here into the unity of a given event, while at the same time retaining their unmergedness.[21]

Bakhtin's idea of Dostoevskian polyphony became the cornerstone of a whole set of theories on "dialogical" writing and thinking, with implications in the arts, communication theory, philosophy, and allied disciplines. Bakhtin's thought, long suppressed in the Soviet Union, is now extremely popular in American academic circles. Bakhtin is describing a special feature that really does exist in Dostoevsky's works, and yet it would be a mistake to overstate the case. The fact of the matter is that we know perfectly well where the author stands in Dostoevsky's works. We *do* have an authorial viewpoint, and it is dominant. Opposing ideas are ridiculed—nihilist arguments are put into the mouths of characters like Luzhin, who is vile, or Lebeziatnikov, who is ridiculous, and it is clear that the implied author sides with the ex-nihilist friends when they react with revulsion and rage to the shibboleths Luzhin parrots.

Properly understood, what polyphony means is that ideas are taken seriously in Dostoevsky's works, and the clash of ideas is portrayed with intense realism and special vividness. Opposing ideas, even those argued against, are presented with insightful characterizations of their proponents, not in Luzhin's case perhaps, but certainly in Raskolnikov's, and even to a degree Svidrigailov's, and we can see something of where those ideas come from and what it feels like to believe them. As one critic puts it, "Each character in Dostoevsky inhabits his own world and not the author's."[22]

Perhaps the stumbling block is the term "fully valued." To say that Raskolnikov's voice is "fully valued" in *Crime and Punishment* is not to say that his ideas are accepted as valid. Bakhtin states:

> The new artistic position of the author vis-à-vis the hero in Dostoevsky's polyphonic novel is a consequent and fully realized dialogical position which confirms the hero's independence, inner freedom, infinalizedness and indeterminacy. For the author the hero is not "he" and not "I," but a full-valued "thou," that is, another full-fledged "I" ("Thou art"). The hero is the subject of a profoundly serious actual dialogical mode of address, as opposed to a rhetorically acted-out or conventional literary one. And this dialogue—the "great dialogue" of the novel as a whole—takes place not in the past, but now, in the present of the creative process. It is, however, not a stenographic report of a completed dialogue which the author, no longer a participant, views from the commanding height of his authorial position: such an approach would immediately turn a genuine and unfinalized dialogue into the objectivized and finalized image of a dialogue, common to every monological novel. The great dialogue in Dostoevsky's work is artistically organized as the unclosed entirety of life itself, of life on the brink.[23]

The idea of dialogue is the key. Dostoevsky's characters are so intellectually vivid that they engage Dostoevsky himself, and us the readers, in dialogue. The idea of polyphony works better for some of the later novels like *The Idiot* or *The Brothers Karamazov*, in which the characters whose voices echo Dostoevsky's own are seriously challenged by some magnificent characters with opposing voices.

Once again it is Dostoevsky's peculiarly well-designed narrative scheme that provides the key. Because we see the events of the novel from a vantage point inside Raskolnikov's head, his abhorrent idea—and the idea of murder certainly is abhorrent to the vast majority of readers—becomes familiar to us, and we begin to feel at home with it. It is not that it is given equal weight or value with the clearly implied authorial stance that murder is wrong, but it has become a part of our world and we view it subjectively rather than objectively.

"For Dostoevsky the important thing is not how the hero appears to the world, but most importantly, how the world appears to the hero and how the hero appears to himself."[24]

In fact, this is a good place to note that the narrative scheme has been changing as the novel has progressed. In part 1 it seemed that everything was visualized from the mind of Raskolnikov (after all, many of the other major characters had not yet made an actual appearance) even if the narrative was in the third person. In the sections that follow, we begin to get glimpses inside the minds of a few other characters. Chapter 3:2 opens with Razumikhin alone, thinking over his new relationships with Dunya and her mother, and the scene with them that follows takes place in Raskolnikov's absence. Chapter 4:3 opens with a lengthy section from the point of view of Luzhin, of all people, after his meeting with the Raskolnikov family. And we get a good deal from the point of view of Svidrigailov later on.[25] What is particularly interesting in the cases of Luzhin and Svidrigailov is that these are the other two characters who express strongly negative ideas in the novel. Even though there is never any doubt about the negative authorial attitude toward their ideas, we do crawl inside their skins just enough to view their idea systems subjectively, to feel what it is like to hold those ideas.

Another way of viewing polyphony is to note, as Bakhtin himself does, that Dostoevsky's characters, the most interesting of them anyway, are often in dialogue with themselves, or rather, that their dialogue with others represents a changing attitude toward the self and one's own ideas. As one critic put it, Dostoevsky is the first writer to dramatize indeterminacy in character, creating hyperbolic suspense.[26] Characters like Raskolnikov and Svidrigailov are working out their own terrifying ideas, and again, we see this from inside. To turn to Bakhtin again: "The idea, as *seen* by Dostoevsky the artist, is not a subjective individual-psychological formulation with a "permanent residence" in a person's head; no, the idea is interindividual and intersubjective. The sphere of its existence is not the individual consciousness, but the dialogical intercourse *between* consciousnesses. The idea is a *living event* which is played out in the point where two or more consciousnesses meet dialogically."[27]

One might even say that Dostoevsky's characters are in dialogue with their ideas, for ideas have active force in Dostoevsky; they seem personified as beings. For instance, Raskolnikov, in part 1, keeps referring to his criminal project as "it" and treating it as though it were an independent will, holding his own will in check: "Am I really capable of *that*? Is *that* really a serious thing?" (1:1); "I will go to [Razumikhin] . . . I will go the next day after *that*" (1:5). And then there is the preponderance of passive verbs describing Raskolnikov's actions in the murder scene. If ideas in Dostoevsky's world are demons, or at least spirits, then our thought is a dialogue with them.

Along similar lines, it may be meaningful to talk about the author's dialogue with himself. Freud thought that fiction writers created their characters out of fragments of their own egos. If this is true, then Dostoevsky is dramatizing his own inner quandaries when he places his characters in dialogue with each other. Certainly his own struggle to believe is dramatized in some of the religious dialogue in his works (particularly in *The Brothers Karamazov*), and in all of his work the "underground" of unconscious drives counterpoints the traditional ideas that he avowed on the surface. He was a writer in dialogue with himself.

In all these ways, polyphony is a valid concept, even if there is never any doubt about the authorial deprecation of some of the ideas presented by the major characters of the novels.

## THE DETECTIVE

No tradition of the detective novel existed in Russian in 1866. The prototypes of the genre, Wilkie Collins's *The Woman in White* and *The Moonstone*, were barely coming out in English during the 1860s. There had been novels with detectives in them; some interesting parallels may be drawn between Porfiry Petrovich, our detective in *Crime and Punishment*, and, for instance, Javert, the police investigator in Victor Hugo's *Les Misérables*. But the tradition did not exist as such, and it would be a mistake to try to fit *Crime and Punishment* into it retrospectively. In a way, Dostoevsky's last novel, *The Brothers Karamazov*, fits into the tradition better, since there, at least, we do not find out until late in the novel who committed the crime.

A number of features make it impossible to consider *Crime and Punishment* a detective novel. To begin with, the murder is committed first thing, by a character we know pretty well, and in fact we see it happen. The primary focus of our attention is on the psychological, existential, and spiritual "punishment" for the murder, and of course this brings us into contact with a whole host of issues completely foreign to the murder mystery: the fate of the Marmeladovs, Sonya's impact on Raskolnikov, Dunya's romantic difficulties, Svidrigailov. This novel may be considered a "mystery" in the religious sense far more readily than in the literary one.

Moreover, the detective is wholly un-detectivelike: he is a mild-mannered, short, slightly pudgy, somewhat effeminate man who appears to be completely scatterbrained (note the "appears"; it is quite possible that his presentation of himself is an act, but an act so thoroughly assimilated that it seems to have become a part of the "real" personality). Here is how Porfiry Petrovich (we never know his last name) is described the first time we meet him:

> Porfiry Petrovich was dressed for staying at home, in a dressing gown, with spotless linen and worn slippers. He was a man of about 35, somewhat shorter than average, thickset and even with a bit of a belly, clean shaven, without moustache or sideburns, with closely trimmed hair on his large round head with its prominent rounded crown. His pudgy round snub-nosed face was a sickly dark yellow, but it was fairly lively and even ironic. The face would have even seemed kindly, had it not been for the expression of the eyes, with a sort of liquid, watery gleam, covered by eyelashes which were almost white, with a twitch, just as though he were winking at someone. Something about the gaze of those eyes was oddly dissonant with his whole figure, which had something of the peasant

woman in it, and gave him a much more serious air than one would have expected from the first glance. (3:5)

(With regard to Porfiry's "womanishness" and his ironic wink at Raskolnikov, remember that Alyona Ivanovna, also a *bába* ["old peasant woman"], seemed to be mocking Raskolnikov just before the moment of the murder.)

To be sure, an unlikely detective is encountered in some of the best detective fiction: the violin-playing cocaine addict Sherlock Holmes, the kindly priest Father Brown, the fussy Frenchman (in English novels, mind you) Hercules Poirot, the British maiden aunt Miss Marple, the closet poet Adam Dalgliesh. Once the tradition of the detective novel is established these departures can be tolerated, even welcomed as interesting variations. But *Crime and Punishment* is more properly a predecessor of the detective tradition than a part of it.

By far the most interesting thing about Porfiry Petrovich is his psychological method. He seems to have determined early on that Raskolnikov is the murderer (once again "seems," for we never get inside this character's mind in the slightest way; we may only infer what he is thinking from his endless blather). He applies psychological pressure to Raskolnikov with the apparently benevolent aim of extracting a confession and initiating an experience of redemption through suffering. More than anything else he exerts pressure by involving Raskolnikov in the process of detection through psychology. He focuses on what it must have felt like to commit the murder, what kind of person would do the thing. Although his questions always remain in a hypothetical third person, the second person is always implied: "What did it feel like when you planned and committed the murder?" Perhaps it is no coincidence that one finds oneself using the terminology of fictional narrative technique ("third person") in talking about Porfiry, for Porfiry's technique with Raskolnikov is very like the narrator's technique with us as readers: both narrator and detective are trying to place their interlocutors into the mind of the murderer. If in Porfiry's case this is complicated by the fact that Raskolnikov really *is* the murderer, remember that we, too, as readers, have become accessories to the crime by our identification with Raskolnikov. The novel wants us to accept universal guilt and to seek redemption, just as Porfiry wants Raskolnikov to accept individual guilt and to confess. Porfiry is the novelist's helper in his moral task. If it may be said that the author has a godlike role in his fictional world, one could go on and say that, just as the narrator is God's servant in the aesthetic sense, so Porfiry is God's servant in the more properly religious sense.

So Porfiry involves Raskolnikov in the process of detection. He drags out the prevalent theories and discusses them with Raskolnikov from a psychological perspective. Razumikhin (Porfiry's distant relation) has already begun this process in part 2, when he scoffs at the idea of the house painter Nikolai as a suspect, precisely for psychological reasons. No one who had just committed murder, particularly of Nikolay's age and background, could be in a frame of mind to behave as Nikolay behaved. He is either innocent or a consummate actor, and he is obviously not the latter. Razumikhin's technique here is that of Porfiry and the narrator: to explore what it feels like to murder.

Porfiry blathers on about irrelevancies, putting Raskolnikov at his ease, delicately removing his defenses, then returns abruptly to the most troubling questions of all, apparently hoping to elicit a breakdown and a confession. Indeed, his whole demeanor, so unlike the aggressiveness we expect from a policeman (and get from Ilya Petrovich, "Officer Gunpowder"), may be seen as a device to put the suspect at ease in preparation for "the kill." In fact, Porfiry's speech is so disarmingly odd that it is virtually impossible to translate without losing its individuality. His language is peppered with obsequious little suffixes—the hissing sound that cringing Russian functionaries used to put on the ends of words and phrases when toadying to superiors—it's not quite "sir" but suggests it. He is constantly using diminutives—those untranslatable suffixes that literally mean "small" but in fact say nothing about the size of the object in question and everything about the speaker's wish to be cute and to endear himself. Although not quite so strong, diminutives produce an impression not unlike the feeling that one gets in English if one calls a book a "bookie-wookie." At the close of 3:5, as Raskolnikov and Razumikhin are preparing to leave, Porfiry babbles on ingratiatingly for a moment, then suddenly slaps his forehead and seems to remember a question he had wanted to ask. It has to do with what Raskolnikov saw at the pawnbroker's apartment when he pawned his watch, but the question is in fact a trap to get him to reveal that he was there on the day the murder was committed. Despite the disarming presentation, Raskolnikov detects the trick and evades it, but it takes a lot out of him—the desired effect.

At their next meeting (in 4:5, if I may permit myself to get a little ahead), Raskolnikov confronts him with this. Porfiry lets the subject drop at first, but then returns to it and admits, in his own inimitable way, that this is his method.

> "And with regard to our 'juridical methods,' as you were so successful in wittily expressing yourself, well, I'm completely and fully in agreement with you, my good man. What suspect, tell me, even from the most benighted peasantry, doesn't realize that first of all, for instance, they will begin to use trivial questions to 'hypnotize' him (to use your happy expression), and then suddenly whack him on the head, just as though with an axe-butt, right on the head, to use your happy metaphor," he sniggered, "so you really thought that I wanted to use the apartment to . . ." More sniggering. "You're an ironic fellow. Well, I won't."

And he proceeds to do so—that is, to use the topic of the apartment to break Raskolnikiv down emotionally. So one of Porfiry's devices for getting inside Raskolnikov's head is to bring Raskolnikov inside his own, to let him see the structure of his investigative work at every point. This is so unnerving to the subject that it has the desired effect.

Of course on a literal linguistic level, Raskolnikov's "expression" is the word "hypnotize." But everyone present (Raskolnikov, Porfiry, narrator, reader) knows that in a more elemental, physical way, Raskolnikov "expresses himself" by a "whack . . . with an axe-butt, right on the head." Once again the parallels between narrator and detective come to the surface. And his methods are so devastatingly precise and effective that it is hard to believe that they are the blatherings of a scatterbrained fool, as they at first appear to be, and not the smoke screen of the cleverest of actors.

## THE ARTICLE ON CRIME

The principal topic of discussion at the first meeting between Raskolnikov and Porfiry Petrovich, with Razumikhin present, is an article "on crime" that Raskolnikov wrote some months earlier. Now there are some strange things about this article in the structure of the novel. The article contains some of the chief rationalizations for the murder, one might even say its ideological foundation. And yet there is no mention of it in part 1, where Raskolnikov is planning the crime and talking about the inception of the idea. We as readers first hear about the article when Porfiry brings it up in 3:5, and Raskolnikov claims to have been unaware that it was published—indeed he almost seems to have forgotten that he had written it.

There are two possible answers to this conundrum, each from a completely different perspective, and both possibly correct. From the perspective of the novel's credibility as a realistic psychological narrative, one could take a psychoanalytic stance and say that repression is taking place. Raskolnikov has forgotten the article because he has buried it in his unconscious mind, repressed it. It is difficult to see why he would repress the *justification* for his crime, unless because of some sort of guilt feeling or "will-to-suffer" he desires to be caught and punished. And indeed this may be the case.

From the perspective of the composition history of the novel, it is hard to escape the conclusion that Dostoevsky simply did not think of the article until after parts 1 and 2 were published. The first mention of the article in the surviving notebooks can be dated after the publication of part 1, so this hypothesis seems plausible.[18] As has already been suggested, these two possibilities are not mutually exclusive; both may be true. They deal with two completely different types of causal explanation: the history of the novel's composition (efficient cause, to use Aristotle's categories once again) and its psychological verisimilitude or credibility (final cause).

Mention has already been made of the prevalence of interpolated narratives in Dostoevsky. The article on crime may be viewed as an interpolated narrative of a sort, although, oddly, we never read it as a text but only hear characters discussing it. This is not a unique instance within Dostoevsky's novelistic universe. At least two other instances come to mind of texts outside the novels that are described and discussed in the novels but never actually appear, although their ideas are of central importance. In *The Devils* a populist (that is, a second-generation nihilist) outlines his book on social theory, which turns into an unwitting reductio ad absurdum of populist theory. And in *The Brothers Karamazov* the famous "Legend of the Grand Inquisitor" is a text described at length by its author, Ivan Karamazov, and discussed with his brother Alyosha. And both of these interpolated narratives (or interpolated discussions about absent narratives) are tied to Raskolnikov's article on crime in an important way: all three texts see at the base of society a fundamental distinction between two groups, a small elite of strong, willful, controlling individuals and a large group of sheeplike followers. This view of society, at least of unredeemed society, as divided into leaders and led, is fundamental to the sociological theory implicit in all of Dostoevsky's works. The tyranny of the strong over the weak is one of the fundamental problems of human existence for Dostoevsky, and I return to it at length later on.

It is also interesting to take a look at the article from the perspective of the journalistic milieu of St. Petersburg during the 1860s. Porfiry Petrovich informs us that the article has come out in *Periodical Discourses*, but Raskolnikov avers that he submitted it to *Weekly Discourses*. Neither journal actually existed, although both names are plausible journal titles for the period. In fact, the "fat journals" were the basic forum for intellectual discourse at the time. They published novels in serialized form (*Crime and Punishment* itself was coming out serially in the *Russian Herald*, along with Tolstoy's *War and*

## Part 3

*Peace*) and articles on social and intellectual questions. The literary works often provided more interesting commentaries on the burning questions of the day, since it was safer to imply things in literature than to say them directly in expository prose. It was not at all uncommon for journals to be closed by the censor for publishing a daring opinion. We are told that this is what happened to *Periodical Discourses*, causing it to send Raskolnikov's article off to a sister (or successor) journal (without informing the author). Indeed, Dostoevsky's own journal, *Time*, had been closed for speaking out too bravely on the issue of the Polish rebellion (and *Time* was not even all that liberal—basically their middle-of-the-road position had been misunderstood, just as with *Periodical Discourses*). *Time* had been succeeded by a virtually identical journal, the *Epoch*. The information about the journals is a perfectly credible account of intellectual life in St. Petersburg at the time. Other details of *Crime and Punishment* give a good picture of Petersburg's journalistic life: Luzhin's fear that he would be denounced in the liberal press was a sensible one—such denunciations were frequent and often devastating; Raskolnikov browses some periodicals in the Crystal Palace and finds mostly stories about fires—indeed fires of any sort had been a "hot" topic since 1862, when nihilists were accused of arson.

The gist of Raskolnikov's article (or of the part that interests Porfiry, which Raskolnikov insists was a side issue) is that exceptional individuals may commit crimes for the benefit of humanity, that the end justifies the means. This, too, had been a hot topic in the press since the publication in 1865 of a *History of Caesar*, by Napoleon III, the nephew of Napoleon I, putting forward this same idea. As has already been noted, this idea is not a tenet of nihilism but a corollary of its basic utilitarian axiom that ethical behavior is to be determined not by religious law ("superstition") but by the scientific principle of the greatest good for the greatest number. Everything we have seen up to this point suggests that Raskolnikov has already left nihilism behind. He has attacked Luzhin's version of utilitarian theory, and he has tacitly acquiesced while Razumikhin has poured scorn upon the movement. At the very meeting in question, with Porfiry Petrovich,

75

Razumikhin attacks the nihilist theory that crime is a result of the environment and as such can be excused. Raskolnikov offers no objection, although if his article on crime was truly in the nihilist spirit he ought to support the theory Razumikhin is attacking. So it seems that Raskolnikov no longer believes in the ideas he had put forward in his article. This may be why he has repressed his memories of the article itself.

The social and intellectual gist of the article has been rejected and repressed, but its personal meaning, the idea that special individuals may overstep traditional moral rules for the good of society, has taken on enhanced importance for Raskolnikov, for he must prove that he is just such a special individual. This aspect of the article lays the groundwork for the existential or Napoleonic motive for Raskolnikov's crime—the need to prove that he is a special individual, a Napoleon; the need to prove his manhood through crime. And this is precisely the psychological detail that Porfiry Petrovich fastens upon. Porfiry proceeds to analyze this issue using the method characteristic of him. Granted that such an idea exists, what must it feel like to believe in it? Would not one attempt to prove one's theory through, well, crime?

"All of these various practical instances are still bothering me!" Porfiry complains. "What if some man or youth imagines that he is a Lycurgus or Mahomet . . . —a future one, of course—and sets about to remove all of the obstacles . . . ?" Raskolnikov concedes that "there certainly must be such cases . . . particularly among the younger generation." Next, Porfiry narrows his focus and zeroes in for the kill:

> "Well, then, when you were composing your little 'piece,' well, couldn't it have been," he sniggered, "that you thought yourself, well, just a teensy-weensy bit, to be just such a 'special' person, with your own *new word* to speak, . . . . And if so, my good man, then couldn't you yourself have decided, well then, in view of some of life's little disappointments and frustrations, or for the benefit, somehow or other, of all mankind,—to stride across some kind of boundary or other? . . . Well, for instance, to kill or rob someone . . . ?" (3:5)

This is reminiscent of *Notes from Underground,* where this very logic is used to posit the plausibility of a literary character: "[Such] persons . . . not only may, but must exist in our society, if one takes into consideration the conditions that have shaped it." Once again, Porfiry's technique turns out to be close to the heart of the implicit authorial stance in this and other novels by Dostoevsky. Even Porfiry's comments about the inevitable suffering of the extraordinary man who commits crime for the public good come very close to statements by Dostoevsky—in this case, statements about Turgenev's Bazarov that Dostoevsky made in the nonfictional *Winter Notes on Summer Impressions.* In a whole host of ways, then, Porfiry Petrovich may be seen as the author's double in the text of the novel itself.

## DREAM REENACTMENT

Part 3 ends with a dream reenactment of the murder. In the interior monologue leading up to this dream, Raskolnikov's thoughts reveal some interesting connections between certain characters. He states the existential or Napoleonic motive in terms of the dichotomy: "Am I Napoleon or am I a bug?" (The Russian word literally means "louse," and some translations read that way, but since that word has completely different connotations in English, let us use "bug," which, for an American, calls up the images Dostoevsky wants here). When he has spoken of his victim, the pawnbroker, he has called her a bug. Now he uses the same term for himself: "Yes, I really am a bug—he continued, latching on to the thought with spiteful glee, digging into it, toying with it and taking great pleasure in it." If he is not a special individual who can commit crime without guilt, a Napoleon, then he is on the same level as his disgusting victim, a bug. He is beginning that identification with his victim that will be an important part of his redemptive suffering.

The following passage also reveals some interesting character linkups: antecedents in this entire paragraph are quite unclear, and this creates confusion about who is being talked about at any given point. But the confusion is Raskolnikov's, and it tells us something important about him. Logically, and grammatically, the italicized "she" could refer to his mother or sister, but in either case the meaning is unclear ("My mother should be just like me—hence I can imagine how she would feel if I embraced her and confessed the murder"; "my sister should be just like me—that's why it's wrong for her to sacrifice her future for mine"). Neither is fully satisfactory from a logical point of view. But then Raskolnikov is not thinking logically; he is "thinking intensely, as though struggling against the delirium that had seized him." In terms of the stream of his consciousness, it makes more sense for "she" to refer to one of the murder victims, since in the paragraph immediately preceding, he has just admitted a connection between himself and the first victim ("The pawnbroker should be just like me— we are both bugs"). The second crucially unclear antecedent occurs when he says, "Oh, how I hate the old woman!" The most recently mentioned old woman is his mother, and he has just confessed hatred for her. It is only when he goes on, "It seems to me that I would kill her again if she were to regain consciousness," that we realize that he is referring to the pawnbroker. Actually what he is doing is establishing a connection between them.

On the right is a "translation" of this paragraph that looks only at the progression of characters and the progression of emotions:

"Mother, sister! How I loved them! Why do I hate them so now? Yes, I hate them, physically, I can't bear to have them near me. . . . A while ago I went up to my mother and kissed her, I remember. . . . To embrace her and to think, 'what if she knew? then. . . .' Could I really tell her at a time like that? That's just what I might have to do . . . Hmmm! *She* must be just like me, he added, thinking intensely, as though struggling against the

Mother—
Sister—
[recollection
of love—
current
hatred]—
Self—Self
identified
(potentially)
with all four
female
characters—
[intensity,
delirium]—

| | |
|---|---|
| delirium that had seized him. Oh how I hate the old woman now! It seems to me I'd kill her again if she regained consciousness! Poor Lizaveta! Why did she have to come back! . . . It's strange, however, why do I practically never think of her, just as though I hadn't killed her? . . . Lizaveta! Sonya! Poor, gentle creatures with gentle eyes. . . . Dear women . . . Why don't they weep? Why don't they moan? . . . They give everything. . . . Their gaze is so gentle and quiet . . . . Sonya, Sonya! Silent Sonya!" | Old woman (mother or pawnbroker)— [hatred, murderous intent]— Lizaveta— [absence of murderous intent]— Sonya—[pity, love]. |

The character progression is from older women who constrain him, through the murderous self, to younger women who give up everything. The emotional progression is from hatred, through murderous intent, to pity and then love. This paragraph is an emotional outline of the novel.

Some scholars have argued persuasively that Raskolnikov's act of murder is in fact a veiled attack on his mother. This connection is not so bizarre as it first seems. Remember that in 1:3 and 4 the letter from his mother was one thing that pushed Raskolnikov toward the murder. He was enraged that the letter, and in particular Dunya's act of sacrifice in marrying Luzhin, obligated him, made him beholden to his family. We have already seen that Raskolnikov likes to be a benefactor but hates to be a beneficiary. Is it too much to suppose that his rage at being placed in this position drives him to murder? Perhaps not.

Likewise the pairing of Sonya and Lizaveta is quite germane, and will be a continuing theme in later sections of the novel. Lizaveta was a meek woman, like Sonya. "She's agreeable to everything," said the unnamed student in 1:6, speaking of Lizaveta, and he goes on to reveal that she is always pregnant, which links her with sexual activity, also characteristic of Sonya. In the drafts, an autopsy reveals her to be characteristic of Sonya. In the drafts, an autopsy reveals her to be pregnant at the time of the murder (the child is said to be Zosimov's).[29] These details from the rough drafts make explicit some of the symbolic connections between characters that are unstated, but implicit, in the novel itself. (See chapter 8 for further discussion of the symbolic connection between murder, sexuality, and birth.) In death Lizaveta is also meek, accepting the blows of Raskolnikov's axe with childlike gestures: "[Her] lips were twisted just as piteously as with very little children, when they begin to be frightened by something, and look intently at whatever is frightening them and get ready to start crying. . . . [S]he did not even lift her hand to defend her face, . . . but merely raised her free left hand slightly . . . and slowly extended it forward toward him, as though pushing him away" (1:7). A similar child-likeness is attributed to Sonya in her early appearances (2:7, 3:4). This pairing of Lizaveta and Sonya, the meek, self-denying sufferers, will take on even greater importance in succeeding chapters.

We proceed to the dream reenactment, in which everything is as it was before, except that there is no sound. Sound comes into play only when he finally makes out the victim's face and sees that she is laughing. (Was Hitchcock thinking of this passage when he created the final scene of *Psycho*? The visual details and positions of characters are different, but the dramatic effect is strikingly similar, as the face suddenly becomes visible.) The victim's laughter, and the now audible laughter of the multitudes who now appear, bring the dream to its horrifying conclusion. And when he awakes, the horror contin-. ues, for the character who now appears, Svidrigailov, turns out to be a grisly double of Raskolnikov himself.

# 7

# Part 4

## THE ABSTRACT PLOT

By the middle of the novel the murder has almost become a subplot, submerged in Raskolnikov's mind, surfacing only when events, other characters, or extraneous incidents bring it into his consciousness, and ours. The surface events of the novel have taken over by this time, and the structure consists of alternating scenes from the novel's various secondary plots and from the seemingly random life of St. Petersburg's Haymarket slum. Raskolnikov remains at the center, but it is his relations with family and acquaintances that provide the alternating scenes, serving to hide, and at the same time to intensify, the submerged tension we feel over the issue of whether or not he will confess. These alternating incidents are juxtaposed against each other, not so much to further the plot or plots on a realistic plane, but to guide the reader through a series of issues and images close to the novel's central ideological concerns. We may call this the abstract structure, as distinguished from the realistic or dramatic structure. The abstract or thematic structure is an outgrowth of the novel's immersion in the stream of Raskolnikov's consciousness. Belinsky said "Art is thinking in images," and although this is not exactly what he meant, his formulation gives a pretty good idea of what is going on in this novel. The work presents conceptual relationships in aesthetic form.

The term "abstract" also suggests nonrepresentational art, and that, too, gives a good clue to what Dostoevsky is up to. Beyond the level of realistic events portrayed, *Crime and Punishment* is a pattern of relationships between ideas and images, and taken as such it is as abstract as a Kandinsky painting. Any realistic work has this level of abstract form—blur the focus on a slide of a painting by Boticelli or El Greco, and you get a nonrepresentational pattern of color, space, and form relationships. In Dostoevsky, one never loses sight of the realistic structure of the novel, the series of real events, realistically portrayed, that bring the novel to its dramatic conclusion. Yet the heightened interest in stream of consciousness gives the abstract structure more importance. The abstract structure complements, and at times even competes with, the realistic structure. This is why, despite his firm grounding in traditional, straightforward realism, Dostoevsky may be considered a true forerunner of much modern, avant-garde writing in the twentieth century.

The alternation between abstract and realistic structure resolves some of the conundrums about the novel. All events in the realistic plot are also part of the abstract structure. But it does not always work so neatly the other way around. Events that may seem to be irrelevant filler in realistic terms (the attempted drowning in 2:6, the accusation by the shopkeeper in 3:6) or contrived coincidence (the many overheard conversations; details of who lives where) make perfect sense in the context of the novel's thematic structure. In this sense, abstract or thematic structure even takes precedence over realistic or dramatic structure. But in general the two are conjoined and complement each other.

The novel's dreams form a vital part of its abstract structure. Psychoanalytic critics have noted that Dostoevsky's technique of "fantastic realism" is quite dreamlike,[30] and the patterns of imagery found in the dreams echo those of the waking sections, since all form part of Raskolnikov's consciousness. There are four dreams in the novel proper (I discuss the epilogue's one dream later), and three of them describe a beating. In each case a woman or female animal is being beaten by a man: in 1:5 Mikolka is beating the mare; in 2:2 Ilya Petrovich ("Officer Gunpowder," the volatile officer from the police station) is beating Raskolnikov's landlady; in 3:6 Raskolnikov beats the pawnbroker once again in the dream reenactment. This reinforces the idea of aggression, particularly male aggression against females, that underlies the entire novel. Other instances of such aggression in the waking sections include the murder itself (1:7), Raskolnikov's thoughts after "the rehearsal" (1:1), Svidrigailov's alleged beating of his late wife (3:1), Lebeziatnikov's beating of Katerina Ivanovna (we hear about it in 2:2), and humorous references such as Razumikhin's joke on the way into Porfiry's room in 3:5 ("I'll brain you") and Porfiry's pointed reference in 4:5 ("'whack him on the head, just as though with an axe-butt, right on the head, to use your happy metaphor. . .'"). Note that the eyes of the victimized females are often highlighted: the boy Raskolnikov is particularly eager to protect the mare's eyes from Mikolka's lash, and the man Raskolnikov notes that suffering women have soft, gentle eyes (3:6). In 1:2 Marmeladov notes that he cannot bear to look into Katerina Ivanovna's suffering eyes. Thus the themes highlighted in the dreams, and in the abstract structure generally, are always echoed in the realistic plot.

The dream of the oasis (1:6) seems not to fit this pattern. It is a dream of rest and of freedom from the ugliness of immediate surroundings. It occurs almost immediately *before* the murder and presents a striking contrast with his aggression there. Water is central to this dream, and elsewhere water is a symbol of suicide (2:6, 6:6). Although other meanings have been suggested for this dream, it seems most plausible to see it as expressing a death wish. Later in the novel suicide is seen as the alternative to confession for Raskolnikov. Here he is dreaming of the repose that death would afford. Even this "out-of-place" dream echoes the patterns of imagery that form the abstract structure.

I defer further discussion of abstract structure and the idea of situation rhyme until the treatment of part 5, as some important pieces of the puzzle do not appear until that part. But the phenomenon of character doubling—that is, thematic contrasts and parallels in relationships between characters—may be discussed profitably at this point and may be considered as a subcategory of abstract structure.

## CHARACTER DOUBLING

A good deal has been written about the phenomenon of character doubling in Dostoevsky's writings, but the subject is a complex one and not always fully understood. Some critics speak of the double as simply a divided character, whose personality suffers from a split (*raskól*, "schism").[31] But generally speaking a character's double is another character who profoundly affects his/her identity in some fundamental way, an alter ego or other self. But the relationship between the primary character and the double may take several forms. The double may echo elements of the major character's personality or life situation—it is similarity that binds them together. Or, the double may possess qualities that are the opposite of those possessed by the primary character—such contrasting or complementary doubles sometimes seem to be two halves making up a single whole. Often in Dostoevsky these types are mixed, and we have two characters who are opposites in every way save one, but the one similarity concerns an issue vitally important to the primary character's identity at the moment when the action of the novel takes place. This creates between the two an extraordinary bond, which is all the stronger because it is often secret. In some of Dostoevsky's works the double is even a supernatural figure. The chief thing to note is that this subterranean bond, beneath the surface of public life (like Raskolnikov's crime), is of crucial importance to the identity of the primary character. In a sense doubling emerges from the character's own inner dialogue and may be seen as an aspect of polyphony.[32]

Character doubling was not a new phenomenon with Dostoevsky; it has its roots in the Gothic novel and the tradition of horror literature. In fact, as literature began to take an interest in abnormal psychology, identity crises, and the like, the language of ghost stories was often what it first used to express these concerns. Writers like Edgar Allen Poe and Robert Louis Stevenson, along with Dostoevsky, psychologized the theme of the double in the Gothic tradition, making the encounter with the other self a psychic rather than a supernatural event. (Stevenson, in particular, was deeply moved by his later reading of *Crime and Punishment*, and his short story, "Markham," [1887] shows its influence.)

The first clearcut treatment of the double theme appeared in the writing of the German romantic E. T. A. Hoffmann, a master of the Gothic short novel. His novella *The Double* presents the main character's encounter with an exact physical double as a horrific event that produces profound emotional disturbance and, finally, ruin for the main character. The encounter with the self in the outside world is so unsettling that it destroys the self; this fact is not explained in the novella but is simply taken for granted. This is a little difficult for moderns to understand. In an age of every conceivable type of therapy and identity analysis, we have become comfortable, even blasé, about challenges to our identity. Our response to meeting an extraordinary look-alike would most likely be to laugh, not to shriek, faint, or run away. Nineteenth-century man did not see it this way, and the double in nineteenth-century literature is very much a spook. Dostoevsky's presentation of the appearance of a look-alike in his own early novella *The Double* (1846) is a good illustration of this attitude. In the course of a whole chapter of nocturnal wanderings and scene setting, along the lines of "it was a dark and stormy night," the pathetic protagonist continually encounters a mysterious stranger, to whom he always reacts roughly as follows: "he trembled in every muscle, his knees, not strong enough to support him, gave way under him, and he collapsed with a groan." He finally comes face to face with his double in his own flat: "All he had feared and foreseen had now become cold reality. It took his breath away and made his head spin. . . . His hair stood on end and he collapsed into a chair, numb with horror. . . . Mr. Golyadkin's nocturnal acquaintance was none other than himself" (5). The encounter with the mystic double was serious business for nineteenth-century man.

Dostoevsky, Poe ("William Wilson," 1839), and Stevenson (*Dr. Jekyll and Mr. Hyde*, 1886) still treat the double as a spooky creature, but they also begin to treat it as a psychological phenomenon—the double is beginning its transition from ghost to psychotic symptom. Furthermore, both Poe and Stevenson treat the double as a secret, evil self that is contrasted with the good, public self. In addition, Stevenson, writing quite a bit later, introduces another feature typical of the development of the Gothic novel in the late nineteenth century: the mechanism that introduces the "spook" is a scientific one, and the Gothic novel begins to move toward what we recognize as science fiction. In fact the double comes to be "explained" so thoroughly, whether in psychic or scientific terms, that by the early twentieth century, when Joseph Conrad wrote his contribution to the genre, "The Secret Sharer," it has moved completely out of the Gothic tradition. Conrad's "sharer" is a completely explicable, albeit somewhat mysterious, figure, and he is benevolent, not hostile. The chief thing is that he profoundly affects the hero's understanding of his own identity; he becomes a helper on the road to self-knowledge. It was Dostoevsky more than any other writer who contributed to this sort of treatment of the doubling theme.

For all its horrific passages when introducing the look-alike, Dostoevsky's *The Double* begins comically. Gogol had given the subject comic treatment in his story "The Nose," where a part of the self (a comic, yet potentially symbolic part—the nose) becomes detached and starts to confront and challenge the self. Dostoevsky's novella begins similarly, as we see the comically insecure hero taking extraordinary measures to bolster his sense of self. But there is no comedy when the double appears. At first he is only an exact physical double, but in time he begins to double the hero in other ways, usurping his position at work, supplanting him in his relations with his servant, and succeeding in a love relationship to which the hero has only aspired. He does this because he seems to possess all the personal qualities the hero lacks. At first it is suggested that the differences in their personalities will provide a basis for friendly complementation, but the double then moves to replace the hero rather than to support him. So the doubling begins with physical sameness but moves in the direction of psychological difference; and both conditions are seen as equally unsettling.

Throughout, a balance is maintained between humor and horror. The work ends with the hero's insanity, but we never know the degree to which the whole story is his mad fantasy. At times Gothic explanations seem to fit; elsewhere, symptoms of abnormal psychology seem to be operating. The uncertainty over this issue keeps the novel on the borderline between Gothic and psychological literature, and it is one of the things that holds our interest as readers.

*The Double* was a work of Dostoevsky's youth; *Crime and Punishment* belongs to his mature period. Doubling is present, but it has become a more complex and sophisticated tool. It has moved away from the Gothic, except for a few scenic trappings, and toward the psychological. None of Raskolnikov's doubles are ghosts; none could even be mistaken for one, although Svidrigailov sometimes looks and acts like one. Raskolnikov's doubles are acquaintances who reflect in some way or other the most disturbing elements of his private emotional life. The event of chief importance in Raskolnikov's life at the time of the novel, his crime, is completely submerged, completely banished from the world of his public life. All the characters who may be seen as Raskolnikov's doubles are people who somehow echo that private event in the public world: they have committed comparable crimes (Svidrigailov) or have otherwise stepped across moral boundaries (Sonya) or the boundaries of traditional ethics (Luzhin). On the lowest level of doubling they are simply people who *know* about the murder (Porfiry, Razumikhin, Sonya, Svidrigailov, and, yes, even Alyona Ivanovna and Lizaveta—they, after all, know about the murder in the most intimate way possible: as its victims). Knowing Raskolnikov's secret makes these characters reflections of his private identity and sets up the strongest sort of bond between them. *Crime and Punishment* may be seen as a circle of doubles, knowers of the secret, surrounding a central Raskolnikov.

Razumikhin doubles Raskolnikov in a fairly superficial, yet important, way. He is a contrasting double for the most part. His personality is the opposite of Raskolnikov's. He is gregarious, well-adjusted, non-alienated, and he likes to charm, even to woo, old ladies, not kill them with axes. Even his name suggests the fundamental contrast with Raskolnikov: *rázum* means "good or common sense," "wisdom," while *raskól* means "split." Razumikhin is the close friend who complements or completes the intimate opposite. (Such relationships become particularly important in Dostoevsky's next four novels: *The Idiot, The Eternal Husband, The Devils* [or *The Possessed*], and *A Raw Youth*.) With regard to knowledge of Raskolnikov's secret, Razumikhin ought to know it—Raskolnikov tells him about it often enough. Each time he seems to take it in, but then later on behaves as though he does not know. From the perspective of the composition of the novel, one can accuse Dostoevsky of revising his plan in midstream, a vice to which he was susceptible, as we will see in the following chapter. Perhaps Dostoevsky simply savored too much the electric tension between the two friends in the revelation scene, for he keeps repeating the scene and then going back on it:

> "Once and for all: don't ever ask me about anything. There's nothing for me to answer. Don't come to me. Maybe I'll come here. Leave me alone. But *don't* leave them. Do you understand me?"
> It was dark in the corridor. They stood by the lamp. For about a minute they looked at each other silently. Raskolnikov's intent and anguished stare seemed to penetrate into his soul, into his consciousness. Suddenly Razumikhin shuddered. Something strange seemed to pass between them. Some idea slipped from one to the other, a sort of hint, something horrible, ugly, and suddenly understood on both sides. Razumikhin went as pale as a corpse.
> "Do you understand now?" said Raskolnikov with a painfully twisted face. "Go back, go to them." (4:3)

Yet a scene very like this is repeated in 6:1, where it looks as though Razumikhin still has not gotten the message. From the perspective of psychological realism, one could argue that Razumikhin continually represses his knowledge of his friend's crime since he cannot acknowledge in his friend an act that would be so impossible for himself—he cannot accept his friend's ultimate otherness. But that is a supposition. In fact we never see into Razumikhin's mind with enough clarity to know about such things for certain. This is Raskolnikov's novel, after all.

## Part 4

At first glance Luzhin could not be more opposite from Raskolnikov, but in at least two ways he may be seen as a secret double. I have already noted that Raskolnikov's negative response to Luzhin's exposition of utilitarian economic and ethical theory is an attack on an aspect of his own development, namely, the relationship between positivistic ethics and crime. Another link ties them together: both enjoy the role of "benefactor" in a "rescue triangle," that is, both like to see themselves saving a young woman in distress (for example, Luzhin:Dunya::Raskolnikov:Sonya). And yet this very characteristic, the smug enjoyment of his own benevolence, is one of the things that infuriates Raskolnikov most about Luzhin. Once again, his revulsion against Luzhin is a revulsion against an aspect of himself. On the other hand, Luzhin is the only one of the "doubles" who does not know Raskolnikov's secret. In general the doubling bond between them is weak. Luzhin echoes Raskolnikov as a reflection in a puddle. Could that be the reason for his peculiar name (*luzha* = "puddle")?

Raskolnikov has female doubles as well. We have already noticed doubling between female characters in the dream reenactment of 3:6 (Sonya and Lizaveta, Mrs. Raskolnikov and Alyona Ivanovna). And we noticed that Raskolnikov began at that point to identify with his victims, Lizaveta and Alyona, creating another sort of doubling. But the most important female double is of course Sonya.

Sonya and Raskolnikov seem unlike in every conceivable way, yet she, too, has "stepped across" a moral boundary and destroyed a human life, her own, as Raskolnikov is later to note. (The Russian word for "crime," *prestuplénie*, literally means "stepping across," or "transgression.") For Raskolnikov, this one similarity becomes a central bond, dealing as it does with his secret attempt to validate his identity through crime. Thus the doubling between Raskolnikov and Sonya becomes a strong bond.

For Sonya, on the other hand, the similarity between their acts is quite incomprehensible. Sonya's crime was a practical necessity for her; it was the only way to save her family. She has never had any motivation but that, and the idea of a crime committed for an intellectual motivation is not only repugnant, but simply incomprehensible to her. The scene in which Raskolnikov tries to explain his motives, in the face of her increasing bewilderment, is almost comic. She does see her own behavior as sinful, and she believes God will punish her, yet she does not allow this knowledge to deter her from her quite conventional piety. A modern sociologist would say that she experiences cognitive dissonance, that is, she persists in beliefs and behaviors that are mutually contradictory but keeps them in such separate compartments that they can coexist with only moderate personality disturbance.

Another sufferer who is a double of Raskolnikov is Mikolka (Nikolai), the house painter who confesses to Raskolnikov's crime. Mikolka is a member of an Old Believer sect noted for its extreme asceticism. Later on (6:2) when Porfiry tells Raskolnikov about this, he uses the word *raskólnik* ("schismatic") to mean "Old Believer," and it sounds almost as though he is saying "He comes out of Raskolnikov." Here is powerful linguistic evidence that Mikolka has become a double of Raskolnikov. Mikolka has accepted his suffering because of his participation in universal guilt; Raskolnikov's guilt is much more tangible, and he too must accept his suffering.

As his crime brings him suffering, Raskolnikov enters into a doubling relationship with his victims, both the pawnbroker (in the dream reenactment he calls himself "a louse," a term he has used earlier for the pawnbroker) and particularly Lizaveta, his accidental victim. He notes the doubling between Sonya and Lizaveta, and goes on to suggest that he will take on their characteristics: "They're both religious maniacs (*yuródivye*); I shall become one myself—it's infectious" (4:4). His identification with Lizaveta, and hers with Sonya, is dramatically symbolized by the exchange of crosses later on.

## STEPPING ACROSS

It is one of the novel's great ironies that Sonya is the exemplar of Raskolnikov's theory on crime: she is a special person who can step across moral boundaries for the public good and do so without losing her own moral dignity. It is Sonya, not Raskolnikov, who is like Napoleon. The reason she can do this while Raskolnikov cannot is that she does it reflexively, totally without premeditation or rationalization. She is not trying to demonstrate any utilitarian theory. While Sonya and her counterpart Napoleon stride across moral boundaries instinctively, without taking thought for themselves, since their eyes are fixed on the goal, their contrasting double, Raskolnikov, surrounds his act with thought. He murders not really "for the public good" but to prove that he is a special person who can do so. The motive is not public utility but private identity. For Sonya and Napoleon the end *does* seem to justify the means because for them the end occupies the entire field of vision at the moment of the crime. For Raskolnikov, as for Luzhin, the self remains the ultimate object of the act, and thus their behavior seems morally invalid to us.

This line of reasoning ties Raskolnikov to the earlier work *Notes from Underground*, where the narrator declares that self-consciousness is the disease of modern man and proclaims his envy for those men of direct action who proceed boldly without rationalization: "Those people, for example, who know how to avenge their wrongs and generally stand up for themselves—how do they do it? . . . That sort of gentleman rushes straight for his goal like a mad bull charging with his horns down. . . . [I] am positively bilious with envy of such a man. He's stupid, I won't argue about that, but perhaps a normal man ought to be stupid, how do you know?" (*Notes from Underground* 1:3). Raskolnikov may be seen as another illustration of the underground man's dichotomy. In fact, existentialism, which is an outgrowth of these texts, is directly involved here. Existentialism is difficult to define, since it is not so much an idea as a relationship between idea and action. Existentialist theory argues that existence or identity must be authenticated through action. But in the light of Raskolnikov's experiences, and the underground man's, we find that the authentication of existence through action may only take place if it is unconscious, if it is free of theoretical rationalization, if only the goal, and not the means, is in sight. This places the existentialist in an embarrassing position. Existentialist philosophical theory can only be valid if it is not a philosophical theory, that is, if it ceases to exist. The twentieth century is an age of contradictions, and perhaps it is Dostoevsky, more than any other writer, who introduces and foreshadows this contradictory age.

Is it not ironic to place Sonya in a class with Napoleon? This novel is chock-a-block with ironies, and one of the greatest of them is that once we cross that moral boundary into the category of special moral beings, we find it populated not with swaggering aggressors, but with self-denying victims who have taken upon themselves the burden of suffering humanity. Raskolnikov has already sensed this situation in the conversation with Porfiry in 3:5, when he notes that anyone committing crime for the benefit of humanity thereby takes upon himself a burden of suffering. He states that any genius/criminal with a conscience will suffer after his criminal act. Razumikhin quibbles that if crime is truly permitted to such a person, there should be no such suffering. Raskolnikov responds, "Let him suffer, if he pities his victim. Suffering and pain are always required of one with an expansive consciousness and a depth of spiritual emotion." And remember that this idea parallels what Dostoevsky himself had said about Bazarov in *Winter Notes on Summer Impressions*.

Elsewhere in Dostoevsky's work this idea surfaces in the treatment of convicts as "sufferers" in *Notes from the House of the Dead* and *The Diary of a Writer*. Furthermore, the Grand Inquisitor in *The Brothers Karamazov* is just such a self-denying sufferer—his control of his flock, and his reexecution of Christ, necessitates his acceptance of a burden of personal guilt that brings him true suffering. Mikolka (Nikolai) the house painter does much the same thing when he confesses to Raskolnikov's crime in order to "accept his suffering" (4:6, 6:2).

The special person is not the aggressor but the victim. It is the victim who has mana or spiritual power in Dostoevsky's world. The model, of course, is Christ. The novel implies the question of whether or not the end justifies the means, and although it takes no formal position, perhaps we can say that for Christ, or for the truly Christlike character such as Sonya, it does. We cannot condemn Sonya for her moral turpitude because she is so completely Christ-like. For her there is no crime; all things are lawful for her. Any end that she would espouse would justify any means she would be willing to use.

The device of contrasting doubling brings about an inversion of the aggressor/victim paradigm. The aggressor becomes the victim, and the victim steps across and becomes the special person to whom all is permitted. This can even be seen as an inversion of nihilist ethics, a spiritual version of it, if you will. The self-victimizing character truly sees his or her advantage in the well-being of others, and when such a character commits a criminal act for the good of others, we do not stand in judgment. The implicit conclusion is that even positivistic ethics is redeemed by Christ-like self-denial. This idea is never explicit; in fact, Dostoevsky might not approve of this particular formulation of the idea, but in a sense it lies at the heart of Dostoevsky's quasi-Christian ethical system.

## SVIDRIGAILOV

It is with Svidrigailov that the idea of the double is most fully developed. Apparently he had a real prototype; the notebooks call him "Aristov," after a character in the prison memoirs. He is surrounded with details connected with the Gothic tradition, underlining the emergence of "doubling" from the literature of the supernatural. The fact that we have heard many terrible things about this major character before he actually appears adds much to the suspense surrounding him. He appears (not "enters") at the end of a nightmare, the dream reenactment of 3:6, and Raskolnikov first entertains the idea that his appearance is a continuation of that dream. Note that this is precisely the halfway point of the novel, adding to the character's "centrality." Furthermore his appearance straddles a boundary, not only between chapters, but between parts, meaning that readers must wait for the next monthly installment (in this case it was two months) to find out more. Making readers wait for the next move of a mysterious character is a classic device to heighten suspense. Certain physical details add even more spookiness to the scene: silence and a buzzing fly (Dostoevsky liked this device—he used it again to ghoulish effect in the grisly and beautiful final scene of *The Idiot*).

And yet just what is it that is so spooky about Svidrigailov? He is dapper, jaunty, and good looking, with a wry wit and a talent for repartee. His opinions are paradoxical, not to say downright bizarre, but quite intentionally so, and he expresses them with charming flair and aplomb. In fact, everything about this character is contradictory; perhaps he is the best example of tension between personality and ideology. As a personality, Svidrigailov represents carnality. He is forthright and honest about his sensuality, and seems quite untroubled by guilt (one psychoanalytic critic sees this as the basis of Raskolnikov's attraction to him).[33] Yet the ideas Svidrigailov puts forward have to do with otherworldly matters. He sees ghosts, in particular the spirits of those for whose deaths he is responsible, to wit, his late wife Marfa Petrovna and a certain valet named Philippe. Asking Raskolnikov if he believes in ghosts, he explains that his late wife Marfa Petrovna "deigns to make visits." Likewise, Philippe appeared shortly after his burial and filled Svidrigailov's pipe.

So Svidrigailov's ideas of the spirit world war against his personality, that of the sensualist. To be sure, Svidrigailov is no idealogue; it is hard to call his comments on these ghosts an ideology as such. It is simply that these spirits, his spirits, are part of his current world, even his sensuous world, one might say. "All three times [Marfa Petrovna appeared when I was completely] awake. She'll come in, talk for a minute or so, then she'll go out through the door—always through the door. Just as though I could hear [or perceive] her." He even connects his belief in the spirit world with his peculiar ideas on mental illness: "I agree that ghosts appear only to the sick; but after all, that only shows that ghosts can't appear in any other way—only to the sick. It doesn't mean that they themselves do not exist."

He ties these ideas to his thoughts on the afterlife, although he is fully aware that he is making it all up as he goes along. The following speech appears within quotation marks, even within his larger quotation, and he refers to it as "literature":

# Part 4

"Ghosts are, so to speak, bits and fragments of other worlds, the beginnings of those worlds. To a healthy man, of course, there's no reason to see them, for a healthy man is a more earthbound fellow, and as it happens, he must live only in this world, for the sake of wholeness and order. But once you've gotten sick, as soon as the normal earthly order has been destroyed in your organism, then the possibility of another world begins to be in evidence, and the sicker you are, the more contact with the other world becomes possible, so that, when you die, you go right over into the other world." (4:1)

Another way of saying this is that sick people are special individuals in a way, that they step across some kind of boundary that divides them from the mass of humanity. Even Svidrigailov's thoughts have the same paradigmatic structure as Raskolnikov's.

But what a paradoxical afterlife Svidrigailov's is, an afterlife of the senses, if you will, for the horrors of Svidrigailov's hell are produced by disgusting sensuous details: "Everybody always imagines eternity as an idea that is impossible to understand, something huge, huge! But why should it necessarily be huge? For a change, instead of all that, imagine that there will be just one little room there, a room just like a country steam bath, blackened with soot, with spiders in all the corners, and there's your whole eternity. You know, it sometimes appears to me in that light."

Svidrigailov represents the sensualist's alternative, but his ideas are the most "spiritual" of the novel, outside of Sonya's. (Another paradoxical double, for the otherworldly Sonya is also a sensualist of sorts, by profession anyway, if not by conviction.)

In what way, then, does Svidrigailov double Raskolnikov? Both are murderers in a sense, for Svidrigailov appears to be morally, if not legally, responsible for the deaths of two individuals, or at least we are led to believe this by several characters—with the narrator's complicity. And yet during their first conversation, Svidrigailov is unaware of Raskolnikov's murder. Even so, it is Svidrigailov who presses the issue of their secret similarity in a criminal conscience. He seems to have prescient, not to say supernatural, knowledge of it. "Well, didn't I say that there was some point in common between us? . . . It seems to me

I did say it. Just a moment ago, after I came in and saw that you were lying there with your eyes closed, and you yourself were pretending—right then I said to myself 'This is the very one!'" And later he adds: "Well, didn't I tell the truth when I said that we were like two peas in a pod?" (literally, "one field of berries"). Raskolnikov is in a better position to appreciate their shared blood-guilt, but it is he who resists most strongly the idea that they are doubles. (Another psychoanalytic critic states that Svidrigailov is Raskolnikov's id (*ono*).[34]

Of course Svidrigailov does find out about the murder, and after this point the doubling between the two increases apace toward the end of the novel. Svidrigailov's discovery of this fact comes at the end of Raskolnikov's first interview with Sonya, in which he all but confesses to the murder. The scene is eerie, right down to its chiaroscuro lighting. (This is another favorite Gothic device of Dostoevsky's: a single light source, often a candle, as here, illuminates a scene that is primarily in shadow, creating a visual effect quite like the chiaroscuro in Rembrandt's paintings.) At the end of the chapter the narrative tone changes from the eerie whisper of the conventional Gothic to a tone that is matter of fact, even jaunty. In that tone, the narrator informs us that Svidrigailov has heard the whole thing. This is another trick of the Dostoevskian Gothic, which he uses to good effect in all of his greatest late novels. When Dostoevsky wants to send us reeling with surprise, in a Gothic or suspenseful mode, he will relate frightening developments in just such a nonemotional tone.

A word on narrative point of view is in order with regard to Svidrigailov. Our opinions about him are formed by other characters, particularly Mrs. Raskolnikov, and even Luzhin, and the narrator does not correct them. We think of Svidrigailov as the chief villain in the novel, or perhaps he shares this (dis)honor with Luzhin. Yet he is not guilty of any crime in the legal sense. He may not even be guilty of any crime in the moral sense. Mrs. Raskolnikov, who introduces him, implies that he poisoned Marfa Petrovna, beat her regularly before that time, and of course, besieged Dunya's honor. (This last crime places him in a hoary tradition of villains in literature: middle-aged men who try to seduce governesses—the names Lovelace, Mr. B., Lothario are catchwords for sexual villainy within the novel tradition.) Svidrigailov himself insists that he did not poison Marfa Petrovna; he equivocates on the issue of wife-beating, implying that she encouraged it; he points out that their marital arrangement (in which his affairs were tolerated) was aboveboard, if a trifle unconventional; and he declares, convincingly at times, that his passion for Dunya is genuine. The other death on his conscience is the suicide of his valet Philippe, and we have little more than Svidrigailov's own comments to inform us on this matter. (What would a personality like Svidrigailov do to a servant that would drive the latter to suicide? Whenever we see him with subordinates he treats them with kind solicitude, although he has a propensity to seduce them. Could Svidrigailov have seduced Philippe? Certainly that would fit in with the general idea of Svidrigailov's sexual perversity.)

One hates to be in the position of defending a character who is obviously intended as the novel's villain, but it is worth pointing out that this novel's villains are guilty of no more than mental cruelty and sexual kinkiness in Svidrigailov's case, and intellectual dishonesty, selfish pride, and slander in Luzhin's case. They are guilty of these crimes primarily in the eyes of the hero, who is a murderer, and his friends and relations. In order to keep one's compass true while reading this novel, one ought to remember that the readers' judgments are being manipulated.

# 8

# Part 5

## PUBLICATION HISTORY

*Crime and Punishment* was published in installments in the *Russian Messenger*, a middle-of-the-road literary journal, during the whole year of 1866, quite coincidentally along with installments of Tolstoy's *War and Peace*. Part 1 of *Crime and Punishment* came out in the January issue and its epilogue in the December issue (although publication was usually about a month behind, so that the epilogue did not actually appear until early 1867). But the publication history was not nearly as smooth as these facts would lead one to believe. Current events, censorship, financial problems, and Dostoevsky's habit of publishing early chapters while still writing later ones, all got in the way, and they left their marks on the final product.

During the summer of 1865 Dostoevsky was in some economic difficulty. He was writing a "natural school" novel about slum life in St. Petersburg, called *The Drunkards* (it was to become the Marmeladov subplot), but when he offered the prospectus to a couple of journals, it was rejected. Needing some kind of advance, he signed an agreement with a publisher named Stellovsky, agreeing to deliver a new novel by 1 November 1866 or forfeit a significant portion of his royalties for works already published. It seems clear that neither *The*

## Part 5

*Drunkards* nor *Crime and Punishment* was ever intended for Stellovsky, as they were offered to journals in the early stages of work. Probably the deadline seemed so far away that there appeared to be no need to worry about Stellovsky's novel. But the deadline hung over his head during the entire period of creative work on *Crime and Punishment*, and did have a significant effect on the writing of parts 5 and 6.

In September he wrote to Katkov, publisher of the *Russian Messenger*, with a new idea for a novella, apparently conceived during his late summer trip to Europe. This was *Crime and Punishment*, and Katkov apparently liked it, for he sent an advance, and Dostoevsky's work on the novel proceeded. *The Drunkards* was incorporated at an early stage, and this subplot forms the bulk of the early notebooks. But Dostoevsky had creative difficulties; he could not find the appropriate tone. Finally in late November he threw everything out and began anew. This time the work went smoothly, and he sent the first portion to the printer in December. Everything points to the conclusion—although no direct evidence in the form of a revised draft or a dated statement survives—that a change in narrative point of view finally put the book on the right footing in November and December. There are undated comments in one of the notebooks announcing the narrative change. The September letter to Katkov suggests that everything else was well thought out at that early stage, and yet all of our early drafts are in the first person. A late change in direction requiring a complete rewrite was followed almost immediately by publication with a new narrative perspective that is demonstrably more effective—everything points to the idea that it was the change to third-person narration that put everything right in December 1865.

In any case, parts 1 and 2 were published in the January and February issues of the *Messenger*. Part 3 did not come out in March, however, although the type was apparently set in time. But on 4 April (shortly before the March issue came out), a St. Petersburg student by the name of Dmitri Karakozov attempted to shoot the tsar. It appears that Katkov delayed publication of part 3 fearing that it would be seen as inflammatory under the circumstances. The explanation given for the postponement of part 3 is a flimsy pretext: "The continuation of the novel *Crime and Punishment* is postponed until the following issue, as illness has prevented the author from reviewing the manuscript before printing as he had hoped to do." But apparently there was no fear that the censor would implicate the *Messenger* and Dostoevsky for inciting Karakozov to his assassination attempt through the inflammatory character of *Crime and Punishment*. Two left-wing journals *were* closed in the aftermath of Karakozov's attempt, but the *Messenger* was untouched. (Ironically and, it seems, quite coincidentally, another youthful criminal, even more similar to Raskolnikov than Karakozov was, came on the scene in 1866. His name was Danilov, and he committed a murder in January that was astoundingly similar to Raskolnikov's. *Crime and Punishment*, part 1, was still with the printer, however, so there is no possibility that he was influenced by it. The similarity was the subject of considerable journalistic comment in 1866, however.) Some critics have supposed that following the postponement, Katkov demanded revisions in part 3, but this fact, and the nature of the supposed revisions, has never been substantiated.

Part 3 came out in the April issue, but the May issue once again contained nothing, and this time the problem was more serious: a disagreement between author and editor over the content of part 4, chapter 4. The conflict concerned Sonya's reading of the Gospel. It was considered indecent for a fallen woman to present the message of resurrection. Another complaint was that Raskolnikov defends his action too vigorously; he is not yet repentant enough. This chapter was substantively revised. We will never know *how* substantively, since only the version published in the *Messenger* has come down to us. "The reading of the gospel was given a different coloration," wrote Dostoevsky to Katkov's executive editor on 8 July. Chapters 1–4 of part 4 were published in the June issue. It is conceivable that the changes were an improvement, for in a letter to Katkov (19 July 1866) Dostoevsky admitted that some of the required revisions did make the novel stronger, as they eliminated verbosity.

Part 4:5–6 and part 5:1–3 were published in the July issue, and part 5:4–5 came out in August, but then another obstacle arose: the

# Part 5

Stellovsky contract. Dostoevsky hired a young stenographer named Anna Snitkin and dictated the novel *The Gambler* to her between 4 October and 1 November. (Since he was later to marry Snitkin, it is ironic that this novel is one of his most autobiographical, dealing with his extended affair with Polina Suslov.)

In November he got back to work on *Crime and Punishment*, again with Snitkin's help. Part 6:1–6 was published in the November *Messenger*, and 6:7–8 and the epilogue came out in the December number.

This troubled publication history may be summarized as follows (the months listed refer to the issues of the *Messenger* in which the chapters appeared, not the actual month of publication; issues generally came out about one month after the given date):

January—1
February—2
March—no installment
April—3
May—no installment
June—4:1–4
July—4:5–6, 5:1–3
August—5:4–5
September—no installment
October—no installment
November—6:1–6
December—6:7–8, epilogue

The chronology of publication can tell us some important things about Dostoevsky's method as a writer. Often he uses the peculiarities of serial publication to good dramatic effect, as when he closes an installment with a dramatic scene like the murder. Occasionally he will close an installment with the appearance of a new character, one whom we have been expecting, but then will postpone until the following section any extended treatment of the character's involvement. He does this with the arrival of Dunya and Mrs. Raskolnikov at the end of part 2, and with Svidrigailov's appearance at the end of part 3, and the readers' heightened suspense is easy to imagine, especially since, as it turned out, readers had to wait not one month but two for the continuation of both of these developments.

But there were months when serial publication, in particular his habit of publishing one section while still furiously writing another, caused problems for Dostoevsky. Essentially, he would "write himself into a corner"; he would commit himself to development in a certain direction and then decide later, after publication of an episode, to move in a different direction. The best example of this is the accusation of the unnamed artisan.

In 3:6, just before the dream reenactment, this individual accosts Raskolnikov and accuses him of murder. The effect is chilling, and we expect much to come of it later. But nothing does. At the end of part 4, published three months later, the man reappears. It turns out that he had been present at the scene of the crime when Raskolnikov revisited it in 2:6 and inferred that Raskolnikov was the murderer. He tells us that Porfiry Petrovich had kept him behind the door during the second interview at the police station (4:5), intending to bring him out as a "surprise," when his plans were interrupted by the sudden entrance of Nikolai the house painter. Now, in 4:6, the man retracts the accusation and apologizes.

Readers are usually confused by this incident, but everything becomes clear upon studying the publication history. Dostoevsky is undoing what he had done three months earlier. One does not need to go to the rough drafts to observe Dostoevsky's work in progress; even the published novel is a "work in progress" of sorts.

## SITUATION RHYME

Close to the core of Dostoevsky's method as a novelist is a set of techniques I call "situation rhyme." The term is not original; a number of scholars have described the same phenomenon using different terminology.[35] Situation rhyme is broader than recurrent imagery, although it includes it, as it includes character doubling. Situation rhyme is the repetition of patterns, or paradigms, throughout the novel at various levels of structure. These patterns may be sets of relationships, systems of behavior, or interaction between characters; they may be physical gestures or positions, linguistic structures, parallel ideas; they may cut across boundaries to unite these disparate levels. The paradigms are *echoed* throughout the novel; they are situations that *rhyme*, that follow the same pattern. Situation rhyme is a system of *echoing* as the fundamental structural device in Dostoevsky's novels.

Theorists allied with structuralism are very interested in paradigms. Structuralism as a theory originated in linguistics and has had its greatest successes in anthropology, particularly in folklore studies. Structuralists talk most often about paradigms from folklore that provide a skeleton for a work of literature, patterns that underlie the very core of a novel. They see the interactions between these paradigms as a language of sorts, a system of paradigms that provides a structure of meaning. The most important current variety of structuralism is semiotics, which seeks to define a system of signs, linguistic and otherwise, that are the building blocks of all communication.

This discussion of situation rhyme does not rely on the terminology of either classical structuralism or semiotics; it is not as interested in folklore as is structuralism, nor in sign systems as is semiotics. But it is related to both. Situation rhyme ranges from underlying structures (at the "macrorhyme" level) to semiotic building blocks (at the "microrhyme" level) and occupies all the ground in between. Dostoevsky's work is full of systems within systems and paradigms within paradigms, so that one can see the same thing writ both large and small at the different levels of the same work. Analyzing Dostoevsky is very like playing with *matryóshka* dolls, those nesting figures you can buy in Russian souvenir shops, depicting one plump Russian granny inside another.

Perhaps the best way to illustrate this is to outline one of the primary paradigms that reverberate throughout the pages of *Crime and Punishment*. The place to begin is with character triangles. There are two important triangles that echo all through the novel: the male dependency triangle and the rescue triangle. The male dependency triangle involves an older controlling female, a male, sometimes younger, who is in some way constrained by her, and a young woman of marriageable age.[36] Here are the particulars:

| Controlling Female | Dependent Male | Young Woman |
|---|---|---|
| Mrs. Raskolnikov | Raskolnikov | Dunya |
| Katerina Ivanovna | Marmeladov | Sonya |
| Marfa Petrovna | Svidrigailov | Dunya, others |
| landlady | Raskolnikov | his late fiancée |
| pawnbroker | Raskolnikov | Lizaveta |
| landlady (Pashenka) | Razumikhin | (Nastasya?) |
| Mrs. Raskolnikov | Razumikhin | Dunya |
| Mme Resslich (6) | Svidrigailov | suicide |
| fiancée's mother | Svidrigailov | fiancée (6) |

The classic instance of the paradigm is the mother-son relationship, with a sister completing the triangle, represented at the beginning of the novel by the Raskolnikov family. But it is echoed all over the place. Raskolnikov is indebted to three older women (his landlady, the pawnbroker, and his mother—the last is more of a moral debt, but it does involve a transfer of money), and he gives money to yet a fourth, Katerina Ivanovna, although not out of debt obligation. In the early chapters there are no strong men; men are weak sinners who must humble themselves before dominant women. To use Marmeladov's expression, these are men "with nowhere to go" (1:2). This is obvious in the case of Marmeladov, but even Svidrigailov is economically dependent upon Marfa Petrovna and muses that he might be seen as "a victim" (4:1). Luzhin seems not to be a part of this pattern at first, but even he gets his comeuppance from the ladies in 4:2. The position of male dependency drives Raskolnikov into a frenzy, as we see in 1:3, 4; he must break out of it somehow—and murder is the path he chooses.

Since this is basically a mother-son paradigm, it clearly reflects a preadolescent stage of psychosexual development. The sexuality of the young woman in the triangle is a matter of some concern: either she is actively promiscuous or she is being courted, not to say besieged.

# Part 5

Clearly this paradigm sets the stage for adolescent psychosexual development, albeit of an aberrant sort. Murder and sexuality are symbolically equivalent in the novel, which is just what we should expect if the murder is for Raskolnikov an adolescent initiation rite into adulthood. The male dependency triangle characterizes Raskolnikov's situation at the novel's outset, the infantile stage he must overcome.

Another, perhaps even more important, triangular paradigm is the rescue triangle. The three sides of the rescue triangle are an aggressive male, a woman under attack, and a rescuing male.[37] Here is a list, comprehensive, I think, but perhaps you can find more, of the instances of this triangle in *Crime and Punishment*:

| Victimized Woman | Aggressive Male | Rescuing Male |
|---|---|---|
| Dunya | Svidrigailov | Luzhin |
| Dunya | Luzhin | Raskolnikov/ Razumikhin |
| street girl (1:4) | pick-up artist | Raskolnikov/cop |
| Sonya | customers/ (Marmeladov) | Raskolnikov |
| Luiza I.'s girls | Razumikhin/Zametov (2:3) | (?) |
| the horse (1:5) | Mikolka (dream) | (young Raskolnikov) |
| Alyona I., Lizaveta | Raskolnikov | (Koch, etc./cops) |
| Sonya (5:1–3) | Luzhin | Raskolnikov/ Lebezyatnikov |
| Polechka | future customers | Raskolnikov |
| Marmeladov family | (Marmeladov) | (Sonya/ Raskolnikov) |

(This does not take into account part 6, where all of a sudden Svidrigailov, of all people, starts rescuing everybody—not really a surprise, as he has made his initial moves in this direction as early as part 4, in his first appearance.)

It begins to look as though this is a novel about rescue, in particular rescue from sexual oppression. Notice that most of the major male characters appear in both masculine roles. (Even Lebeziatnikov, the ridiculous nihilist who helps Raskolnikov rescue Sonya from Luzhin's slander in 5:3, has taken the aggressive role at an earlier stage. Marmeladov tells us in 1:2 that he has beaten Katerina Ivanovna and sought Sonya's favors, although the imagery of 5:1 suggests for him a feminized or childlike character. This may not do much for his credibility as a character, but it makes him fit the pattern.) The paradigm operates on all levels, from those central to the novel's plot and meaning, to subplot relationships, to echoes in interpolated narratives. Dostoevsky saturates us with the theme of rescue.

The idea of rescue shows us some important things about Raskolnikov's patterns of thought. Raskolnikov is enraged by sexual oppression—witness his response to Svidrigailov, Luzhin, and the pick-up artist of 1:4. This outrage is one of his motives for the murder—he wants to use his "special status" (and perhaps his booty) to help the oppressed. He is particularly outraged by aggression masquerading as rescue (Luzhin), and by the related phenomenon of rescue for selfish motives (although he may be subconsciously troubled by the fact that his own rescuing activity could be seen as selfish). He relishes the role of rescuer or benefactor (with Dunya, Sonya, the Marmeladovs) but cannot tolerate for himself the role of rescued victim (his mother's letter in 1:3, 4; receiving alms after being accidentally lashed in 2:2). In a sense, Raskolnikov's "punishment" is that he must learn to accept the (feminine) role of rescued victim, and that he must learn this acceptance from meek, downtrodden Sonya, who turns out to be both his rescuer and his model in this regard (a reversal that is both sexual and ethical).

Now rescue triangles are in fact part of a larger system, one I have called the tyrant/victim paradigm, which is a central axis for all of Dostoevsky's work. It involves two opposing stereotypical characters, an aggressor and his victim. The relationship between the two creates a power imbalance in the novel, a dominance hierarchy, to use a term popular in ethology or animal behavior studies. What usually happens in a work by Dostoevsky is that the power balance shifts, the dominance hierarchy is inverted, the weakling takes control. For the victimized character in Dostoevsky has what anthropologists call mana, the mysterious spiritual power possessed by certain holy subjects and personages. In Dostoevsky this power is wielded by the sick or dying individual, the prostitute, the beggar, the effeminate man, the drunkard, the down-and-outer, the abused child, the half-insane person. It is this victim that galvanizes human sensibility, and it is the bully, the Lothario, and the murderer who must ultimately submit to her or his spiritual force.

What happens when we create a third side to this structure—someone to rescue the victim from the tyrant? The Dostoevskian rescuer is in a peculiar position, for he must have enough power to effectively challenge the tyrant. Indeed, he could use this power to become a tyrant himself—in fact, this may represent a powerful temptation for him. He generally possesses some aggressive instincts himself, which he may or may not be aware of. At the same time, his pity for the victimized innocent exerts such a powerful attraction for him that his response may take the form of imitation. So the rescuer is a contradictory character who stands poised between the extreme stereotypes of both ends of the hierarchy, prepared to take any of the roles in the paradigm. He may shuttle back and forth between submissive and aggressive behavior, or he may maintain constant tension between opposing elements within himself. He may, like Raskolnikov, be fairly unconscious of the shifts going on within himself, or he may, like Svidrigailov, be acutely aware and take voluptuous pleasure in every new twist of his sensibility.

The most important symbol for the tyrant/victim system in the corpus of Dostoevsky's work is the act of bowing. Dostoevskian bowing generally involves the tyrant bowing to the victim, and as such the bow often represents the crux of the work, the moment at which the victim gains symbolic or actual dominance over the tyrant. Furthermore, the act of bowing has both an aesthetic and an ethical dimension: aesthetic because it symbolizes the inversion of the dominance hierarchy that forms the novel's turning point, and ethical because the submission of the aggressor to the victim is the beginning of redemption for Dostoevsky. When the aggressor bows to the victim we are at the eye of Dostoevsky's maelstrom, the key to his system of echoing.

There are only two such bows in *Crime and Punishment*; the behavior is more frequent in other works, such as *The Brothers Karamazov*. But the bows of *Crime and Punishment* do form the aesthetic and symbolic heart of the work. There is no mystery about the meaning of these bows. Dostoevsky tells us quite forthrightly, through the mouths of his characters, what these bows mean: they represent the identification and veneration of suffering. "Suddenly [Raskolnikov] bowed down quite quickly and, falling to the floor, kissed her foot. Sonya recoiled from him in horror, as from a madman. And he really did look quite mad. . . . 'It is not to you that I bowed; I bowed to human suffering itself,' he pronounced somewhat wildly, and walked away to the window" (4:4). Raskolnikov is the aggressor bowing to the victim, and the hierarchy of dominance has been inverted with this veneration of suffering. When Sonya bows to Raskolnikov in 5:4, we remember the significance of the earlier act and we realize that she is venerating him as a sufferer. "There is no one unhappier than you, no one, now, in the whole world," she says, and later repeats, "Such suffering!" (5:4; she begins using the familiar pronoun *tebe*, with him only at this point, whereas he has used it with her throughout, apparently because her social position as a prostitute is so far beneath him). Her bow signifies that he has crossed the line to become a special sort of human being, a victimized character, self-victimized in this case, possessing the mana of suffering.

Let us return now to our triangles, in particular, to the relationship between the male dependency triangle and the rescue triangle. The controlling female is absent from the latter, the aggressive male from the former. The male dependency triangle reflects a preadolescent stage of psychosexual development, characteristic of the novel's beginning, while both aggression and rescue are acts of mature males, and this paradigm becomes more important as the novel progresses. Raskolnikov's murderous initiation rite has taken him out of the first triangle into the second.

If we look at what happens in the triangle "Pawnbroker—Raskolnikov—Lizaveta" we see that Raskolnikov has broken out of this intolerable paradigm by destroying it; he has killed both of its other members. But in destroying the paradigm, he has destroyed himself as well. Some critics have even posited the self-destructive "will-to-suffer" as a motive for the murder itself.[38] Raskolnikov has become a victim, his own victim, and now he must be rescued. And it is Sonya, the prototypical victim, who will rescue him, in the classic Dostoevskian way, through the inversion of the tyrant/victim paradigm.

Of course this is not the optimal way to achieve psychosexual maturity. Razumikhin illustrates normative development. He steps into the triangle "Mrs. Raskolnikov—Raskolnikov—Dunya" as Raskolnikov's replacement at the moment when he helps the family rescue Dunya from Luzhin (4:2)—that is, when he acts as rescuer in the adult paradigm. This is the classic fairy-tale pattern (hero kills dragon and wins princess's hand in marriage) that is the backbone of so many novels. It is presented here as the backdrop for Raskolnikov's aberrant pattern. But it is Raskolnikov's pattern that illustrates the aggressive aspects of sexuality that must be neutralized through the submission of the tyrant to his victim.

## MORE RECURRENT IMAGERY

At the microrhyme level, situation rhyme takes the form of recurrent imagery. Mention has already been made of bridges and water.

The image of "stepping across" has its basis in the title and in the existential motive for the murder, but the repetition of the image pops up in the most unlikely places. In 4:2, for instance, Luzhin tells Dunya, "There is a line which it is dangerous to cross, but once you have crossed it, you cannot go back."

The image of childlikeness is strongly connected with both Sonya and Lizaveta, and even a "nongesture" can confirm this through "rhyme" in Dostoevsky. The narrator points out to us that these women, just like children, *do not* raise their hand to protect themselves when attacked: Lizaveta at the moment of the murder (1:7), Sonya at the moment of confession (4:4), and oddly enough, Dunya with Svidrigailov in 6:5.

Another prevalent image in *Crime and Punishment* is the door. Yury Lyubimov's stage version of the work, done first at Moscow's Taganka Theatre and later staged in English translation at Washington's Kennedy Center and elsewhere, aptly places a freestanding door in the upstage center area and frequently places characters on either side of it. The novel is preoccupied with doors and the question of whether they are open/unlocked or closed/locked. Raskolnikov always leaves his door unlocked, even when he is out, to the surprise of Razumikhin and others, while Alyona Ivanovna is careful to leave hers locked, even when she is home. After murdering her, Raskolnikov leaves her door unlocked, with terrifying consequences, and her door is likewise ajar in the return to the scene of the crime (2:5) and the dream reenactment (3:6). He fortuitously finds the janitor's door ajar, enabling him to obtain and later get rid of the axe.

But the most distinctive paradigm involving doors in *Crime and Punishment* is a scene in which characters find themselves on opposite sides of a closed (sometimes partially closed) or locked door. They may both be aware of each other's presence, or one of them may be unaware. This paradigm is stated at the very beginning of the novel, as Raskolnikov sees his landlady peering at him from behind an almost closed door while he leaves for the "experiment" (1:1). Precisely this configuration is repeated at Alyona Ivanovna's during both the experiment and the murder itself. A moment later it reappears terrifyingly as Raskolnikov takes the old lady's place inside the locked door and Koch and Pestryakov take his place outside it. Later on the paradigm is repeated as we learn that Svidrigailov is listening, and will be listening, as Raskolnikov visits Sonya and eventually confesses to her.

The open door represents confession for Raskolnikov. Opening the door to Kokh and Pestryakov in 1:7 would be tantamount to confession. The closed door in 4:4 and 5:4 hides the fact that Svidrigailov is actually hearing everything—that is, that the door is, in a sense, not really closed. Raskolnikov's tendency to leave his door unlocked can easily be seen as evidence of an unconscious will to confession.

Another possible meaning of the open door is that it represents feminine "openness" or promiscuity. This is a novel in which prostitution is rife—the female lead and many of the female extras are whores. Dunya's virginity is constantly under attack. The pawnbroker's apartment is a feminine space—two women live there, one of them promiscuous. Men are constantly knocking, asking to be permitted to enter and leave something in exchange for money. It is not stretching matters too far to see the door to the pawnbroker's apartment as a symbol for virginity and its opposite. Closed door/open door equals virgin/unchaste woman. Sonya's sexual submissiveness, her promiscuity, is her crime, but her spiritual submissiveness, her being Christ-like, is her virtue. Could not the open door symbol be a key to this link as well? When Raskolnikov confesses, he identifies with his submissive (promiscuous female) victim. He is feminized as he rejects aggressive behaviors in favor of submissive acceptance of suffering. It is no accident that the open door represents both confession and feminine sexual submission. These elements are symbolically united in the novel's denouement.

Some of the recurrent imagery is specifically designed to prepare us for the epilogue. When Porfiry mentions Lazarus in 3:5, he is introducing the theme of resurrection that is restated in the first interview with Sonya (4:4). "New Jerusalem," for the leftist circles Raskolnikov has been associated with, meant an earthly paradise, constructed by utopian social thinkers, but in the religious context of *Crime and Punishment* it has quite a different meaning.

Other recurrent images are present; mention has already been made of machine imagery in the murder scene, and it is present in Raskolnikov's scenes with Sonya, which are clearly parallel with the murder. The alert reader may find even more networks of such images.

## ON PHONY CIGARETTE CASES AND CROSSES

Situation rhyme reaches down as far as the linguistic level, the level of specific concepts, words, and even parts of words. Words and word roots that are constantly repeated, completely out of proportion to their actual importance to the movement of the story, seem to take on symbolic stature and pose themselves against the repetitive symbols of the work as part of an overall symbolic structure. This is the most detailed level of microrhyme.

We have already had a look at the repetition of imagery of locked and unlocked doors. The Russian root meaning "to lock" is $p\backslash r$ (with alternating vowels between the $p$ and the $r$, and with various prefixes, most commonly $za$-). Words like $zapór$ ("deadbolt lock") show up fairly frequently, as we would expect. One noun that looks very much like it might be (but in fact is not) related is $topór$, meaning "axe." This is a "false etymology," positing a connection between two objects in the reader's mind, even though no actual etymological link exists. Of course, an axe is the murder weapon in *Crime and Punishment*, so the word crops up fairly often (anagrams for it occur as well: the scandal in 5:3 causes a "hubbub" [$rópot$], and Mrs. Raskolnikov says in 4:2 that Razumikhin is a "lively" [$ras$-$tórop$-$ny$] young man). Raskolnikov conceals the axe under his clothing; indeed, it is rather suggestive dangling there, increasing the likelihood of our conjecture about the symbolic sexual character of the murder and of locked ($za$-$p/r$) and unlocked doors. The device he uses to dangle the axe under his coat is a "loop" ($petlyá$), and he spends almost as much time making this loop as he spends on the phony cigarette case. The more common translation of $petlyá$ is "noose," and this meaning is certainly operative for Raskolnikov the morning after the murder as he tears the $petlyá$ to shreds between periods of delirious sleep. Actually, $petlyá$ can refer to any circular device used to hold another object in place, and, as such, it can refer to the "eyelet" of a deadbolt lock. And sure enough, in 1:7, immediately after the murder, when Koch and Pestryakov are waiting outside the door and Raskolnikov is trembling inside it, the deadbolt ($zapór$) is rattling terrifyingly in the eyelet ($petlyá$), just as Raskolnikov's axe ($topór$) dangles from his loop/noose ($petlyá$) under his clothing. The prefix opposite in meaning to $za$- is $ot$, and consequently a hypothetical opposite (the word does not actually exist) of $zapór$ should be $otpór$, again an anagram of $topór$. If the axe represents masculine sexuality and masculine aggression, and if locking imagery represents feminine chastity, it is easy to see how the two form an opposing pair, both intimately involved in the murder/sexual initiation. These linguistic relationships show the operation of situation rhyme at its most microscopic, sublexical (smaller than words) level, and even here the patterns we have observed in the paradigms of macrorhyme are confirmed.

Another physical object that is given inordinate attention in *Crime and Punishment* is the homemade phony cigarette case that Raskolnikov gives to Alyona Ivanovna as an object to be pawned, to distract her attention before bringing the axe down on her head. The Russian word for a pawned object is *zaklád* (*za-*, "beyond/behind"; *-klad*, "put/place"—"object placed behind or beyond, in a special, perhaps hidden, place"; the root *klad* by itself means "buried treasure," while the verb from *zaklád*, can mean "to close off or block off," relating to the image of closed doors). The word *zaklád* appears with amazing frequency in *Crime and Punishment*, particularly in the early sections. Of course this occurrence is realistically motivated to a large extent—Raskolnikov does in fact steal a quantity of *zaklády* from the pawnbroker. But the word is used in other contexts as well. In particular the expression *bítsya ob zaklád* ("make a wager"), which combines *zaklád* with a reflexive form of the verb *bit* ("to beat, to hit"), is used by Razumikhin and Raskolnikov in 2:6 and 2:7.

And other words based on the same root keep popping up. In 1:2 Raskolnikov muses sardonically as he leaves the Marmeladovs' that "they've found a real gold-mine in Sonya," referring to her sexuality and the profits to be reaped from her sale of it. The word he uses, *kolódez'* ("mine, mine shaft, lode, mother lode; well, spring; any deep and narrow pit") is based on the same root (*klad*) that we find in *zaklád* (note that the consonants are the same—k/l/d). The meaning is vulgar but clear. *Kolódez'* is repeated two pages later in another context (Nastasya uses the word to mean "wellspring"), as though to reinforce the imagery.

The link with Sonya's sexuality may be the key to understanding the special meaning of *zaklád*. Note that both murder victims are women, and remember that they are doubled by two women in Ras-

113

kolnikov's personal, one might even say sexual, life—his mother and his future bride. Note also that the objects stolen by Raskolnikov come from the pawnbroker's trunk (*ukládka*, also from *klad*), which is kept under her bed. Since the murder is a male initiation rite, it becomes increasingly necessary to attribute a sexual meaning to the *zaklád*.

Raskolnikov muses about the cleanliness of the pawnbroker's apartment, noting that it must be Lizaveta's doing (1:1). One chapter later he muses on the particular attention to cleanliness necessary to Sonya's profession, almost in the same breath with his observation that she is a "gold mine" (1:2). Ironically, the word he uses in both instances can also mean "purity, chastity."

Let us take another look at the *zaklád* itself. It is described in extraordinary, and unnecessary, detail in 1:6 as Raskolnikov prepares it for the murder:

> This "pawn" was, however, not a pawn at all, but simply a smoothly sanded wooden block, of a size and thickness no larger than, perhaps, a silver cigarette case. He had found this piece of wood accidentally, on one of his walks, in a courtyard where there was a workshop in a wing of the building. Later he had added to the block a thin smooth metal strip, probably a fragment of something or other, that he also found on the street at that time. Placing both pieces (the metal one was smaller than the wooden one), he tied them firmly together, *crosswise* [*krest-nákrest*; critic's italics] with a thread. Later, he had neatly and stylishly wrapped them in clean white paper and tied the whole thing up in such a way that it would be a job to untie it. This was in order to distract the attention of the old woman for a time, as she would begin fiddling with the knot, and thus give him a moment's extra time. The metal plate was added for weight, so that the old lady, at least for the first moment, would not guess that the "object" was wooden.

The attention to this object is altogether inordinate—any object would do. Not only that, but we are told that Raskolnikov has worked on it in advance, carefully planning its construction. The preparation of this object has obviously been a part of Raskolnikov's criminal project

from an early stage. During the murder scene, Alyona Ivanovna's ex-
amination of it is one of the slowing devices that makes it seem as
though the murder takes place in slow motion. It will even be described again in detail in the epilogue, where we are also told that it
was found by the police clutched in the old woman's hand. Not only
is there no reason for Raskolnikov to go to such lengths to create a
convincing ruse, but there is also no reason for the narrator to go into
such detail in describing it to us.

What is there about the structure of this object that could justify
such an unseemly amount of attention? It has a wooden center and a
metal shell, surrounded by a paper covering. Its structure is that of a
seed. Symbolically, then, we might say that during the murder a seed
is violently placed in the locus of the mother/bride. This may be tied
to other images relating to the murder project. In 1:6 the idea of the
crime is referred to first as a "chick breaking out of its shell" and then
as an "embryo."

Along these lines, a phrase used at the very moment of the murder
is significant. Both Garnett and Coulson say that as soon as the axe
came down, Raskolnikov's strength "returned to him." But the Russian text states specifically that his strength "was born" (*rodílas'*). The
use of the word "birth" at that moment makes the symbolic linkage,
murder/sexual act/conception, more plausible.

If the murder is a symbolic act of coition and conception, and if
this symbolic theme is treated with any consistency by the author, then
something ought to be "born" in the course of the novel, some physical object with a strongly symbolic meaning central to the overall
meaning of the novel. It should come from Lizaveta/Sonya, the victim/
bride, and it should have two parts, one wooden and one metal.

And lo, in 5:4 it appears, in the form of two crosses. One is
Lizaveta's, made of brass, the other Sonya's, made of cypress wood.
"Are you wearing a cross," asks Sonya at the end of 5:4. (Remember
that it was noted in the dream of 1:5 that Mikolka was not wearing
a cross as he beat the mare.)[39] "No, you really aren't? Well, here, take
this one, made of cypress. I've got another one left, a brass one, it was
Lizaveta's. Lizaveta and I exchanged crosses—she put her cross on me,

and I gave her a little icon of mine. Now I'll start wearing Lizaveta's cross, and give this one to you. Take it, it's mine, you know." They finally decide to wait to exchange them until he is on his way to confess. In 6:8 they are duly produced, and Raskolnikov dons his cross. He then says to Sonya, "The brass one, Lizaveta's, the one you'll take, can you show it to me? So it was on her, at *that* minute? I also know two crosses like that one, a silver one and a little icon. I threw them back on the old woman's chest at *that* time." A look back at the murder scene shows that he is not *exactly* right; there are three religious objects on a string around the pawnbroker's neck at the time of the murder: a small icon and two crosses, one cypress, and one brass. The connections between these objects and those exchanged by Sonya and Lizaveta are actually closer than Raskolnikov has supposed. Most important, the extraordinary emphasis on the physical details of these objects, and on which ones belong to whom, and who ends up with what, all tends to confirm what we have discovered about the symbolic connections between the crosses and the phony cigarette case, between the symbolic sex act that is the "crime" and the symbolic birth that attends the "punishment."

So a birth occurs in the novel. The end of the epilogue takes place just nine months after the "body" of the novel. What is it that is born, symbolized by the crosses? Perhaps we might say it is Raskolnikov's soul, perhaps his faith, or at least the possibility of faith in the future; certainly it is his burden of suffering, which is expected to bring him redemption in the future.

Students are often "put off" by such symbolic schemes, particularly if they are sexual in nature. One certainly ought to be wary of launching such an elaborate symbolic pattern. I always advise students against it; it is far too easy to get carried away, especially if you do not read the language of the original. It is of utmost importance to derive all details of the symbolic pattern directly from the text itself. Furthermore, a pattern like this one, based on networks of linguistic detail, is not necessarily thought out consciously by the author. Structuralists, semioticians, and psychoanalysts all agree that our speech, and our texts (written speech), contain patterns that are quite significant despite the fact that we are unaware of them. This is no different for authors than for anyone else.

The truest test of the authenticity of such a symbolic structure lies in the question of whether or not it reinforces other themes that are unquestionably present in the novel. The idea of birth or rebirth is absolutely central to the novel. *Crime and Punishment* is a story of spiritual rebirth or resurrection.

# 9

# Part 6

## THE OTHER PATH

Svidrigailov's role in the novel grows from a rumor in parts 1–3 to a ghoulish presence in parts 4 and 5. His one big scene with Raskolnikov at the beginning of part 4 makes him a tangible figure, albeit still a little ghostly around the edges. And although he never really leaves the stage for the remainder of parts 4 and 5, he never really properly appears on it either. He simply makes an occasional cameo to remind us of his presence, such as the chilling moment at the end of 4:4 when we learn that he has been listening to the private conversation between Sonya and Raskolnikov in her room, and that he will be there next time too. The next time Raskolnikov goes to Sonya's room, we do not even need to be told again that Svidrigailov is listening; we assume his presence, and that is emblematic of the way he hovers in the background throughout parts 4 and 5.

But in part 6 Svidrigailov takes over. More than half of the section is devoted to his activities. In the early chapters he takes over as everybody's angel. As with so many literary events, there can be several different kinds of causal explanation for this, for which distinction Aristotle, once again, gave us a tidy set of terms. The final cause, the novelist's goal toward which all of this tends, is the proper resolution of the novel's plot. If the work is to have anything remotely resembling a happy ending, someone has got to step in and provide for Sonya and the Marmeladov children, saving Polechka and Sonya from prostitution and enabling Sonya to travel to Siberia with Raskolnikov's prisoners' convoy. And someone has got to put the Raskolnikov family finances on a stable enough footing so that Dunya can start turning down the likes of Luzhin and Svidrigailov, and get about the business of living happily ever after with Razumikhin. Svidrigailov steps in and uses his considerable financial resources to take care of all of these items, and for this we all (not the least the Marmeladov and Raskolnikov families) ought to be very grateful to him.

Another "final cause" for making Svidrigailov the angel is that it fills out the rescue paradigm. Every important male character except Porfiry and Marmeladov acts as both aggressor and rescuer in the rescue triangle. It is important for Svidrigailov to step into the rescuing role to complete this pattern.

But there is an efficient cause as well, a proximate psychological reason in Svidrigailov's emotional life. Sadistic personalities often engage energetically in charity, particularly directed toward their masochistic counterparts, their victims. Perhaps it is a way of dealing with feelings of guilt, but this other side of the sadistic personality is just as essential, and just as pleasure producing, as the need to cause pain. So Svidrigailov's charitable work in part 6 is not only a deus ex machina enabling the novel to come out all right; it also presents a believable side of this complex character.

But why, in a novel so preoccupied with Raskolnikov's mental state, and with the issue of whether or not he will confess, is such a large piece of prose devoted to another character, albeit his double, and that, just as suspense is building toward the novel's conclusion, just as he *is* about to confess? The reason is that Svidrigailov represents an alternative for Raskolnikov. He makes this explicit as they come out of the tavern: "Your way lies to the right, mine to the left, or perhaps the other way around." The other path that Svidrigailov represents is, of course, suicide. Suicide is, after all, another sort of "stepping across." Water is the symbol for suicide—this ties in with one of the novel's major symbolic systems, since Raskolnikov's thoughts about suicide up to this point have always involved contemplating water from a bridge. Water as a symbol for death is fully realistic; people really do drown themselves. (Why, then, does Svidrigailov not take his life by drowning? With symbolic systems, as with the personality/social type/ideology system, Dostoevsky likes to add a jarring detail that does not seem to fit, something to keep the pattern from being too neatly allegorical and to make the picture vibrate.) So water stands for death quite realistically, but also symbolically, since suicide for Svidrigailov is a willful plunge, an immersion, or submersion, in another reality, that spidery steam-bath (water, again) that represents the "other world" for Svidrigailov. (He also calls it "America"—which generally represents in Dostoevsky a place so completely other as to be incomprehensible.) Consonant with the water symbol, Svidrigailov's final day in this world is positively drenched. It is raining torrentially, and he crosses bridge after bridge in his last nocturnal perambulations.

He contemplates the water with distaste, but accepts it as necessary. He wants to do the deed in Petrovsky Park (where Raskolnikov had the horse dream of 1:5), which is on a small island by the Túchkov Bridge (across the river from Razmukhin's old apartment), but then he changes his mind and shoots himself in nearby S'ezhskaya Street (the street name suggest two related verbs, both curiously apt, based on the same root/prefix combination, one meaning "to make a trip out of town" and the other meaning "to slither down"). The scene is described with the same macabre matter-of-factness that we noted at the end of 4:4. Present at the scene is a figure so unlikely that we must assume that it was Dostoevsky's intention to make him improbable, perhaps in order to put the scene in even greater relief. He is a Jewish policeman speaking with a strong Yiddish accent. His name, the narrator guesses, again with improbability so outrageous it is obviously intentional, is Achilles, and this echoes the image of classical antiquity already suggested by Svidrigailov's first name, Arkady (Arcadia). The narrator speaks dryly; the policeman provides both comic relief and classical imagery; the leaves are still dripping from the nocturnal downpour; Svidrigailov pulls the trigger. It is the morning of the day Raskolnikov will confess.

What of Svidrigailov's character? I have suggested above that he is sadistic, but in fact our evidence for this idea is pretty flimsy. Mrs. Raskolnikov wants very much for us to think that he beat his wife Marfa Petrovna regularly and was responsible for her death, but we never get much more than innuendo by way of proof. Likewise, his responsibility for the death of his servant Philippe is substantiated only by innuendo, this time his own and, of all people's, Luzhin's (4:2). To be sure, Svidrigailov is a womanizer, and that is enough to place him in the role of aggressor in Dostoevsky's paradigm of sexual oppression. And he has a special interest in little girls, which blackens him even more in Dostoevsky's ethical system. There is the rumor, also presented by Luzhin (4:2), that he raped Mme Resslich's niece, resulting in her suicide (an exact rehearsal of the "Stavrogin's Confession" chapter of *The Devils*).

But Svidrigailov has a submissive side as well (also consistent with the classic sadistic personality). He calls himself a "victim" in his relations with Dunya (4:1). He was beholden to Marfa Petrovna economically, and morally as well, in addition to being younger than she (4:1). At the time of their marriage she had rescued him from debt, then carried him off into the country "like some sort of treasure." He finds all of this quite piquant.

And he experiences something like ecstasy when Dunya holds a gun on him, and shoots him, drawing blood, in 6:5. Like all of Dostoevsky's most interesting characters, Svidrigailov is a mix of aggressive and submissive characteristics. What makes him unique is the degree to which he is aware of his contradictory nature and takes genuine sensuous pleasure, even sexual pleasure, in the contrasts that result. Svidrigailov's function is to make explicit the sadomasochistic complex implied by Raskolnikov's behavior. Sonya, who presents the image of the sexually abused child (she is called childish again and again, and she is forced into prostitution at an early age), is the opposing image that completes this sadomasochistic complex.

Sexual molestation of an underage female is something like a primal crime in Dostoevsky's ethical universe. The most compelling version of it is "Stavrogin's Confession," the chapter of *The Devils* (*The Possessed*) that was initially suppressed by the censor, then discovered and published after Dostoevsky's death. But it is difficult to find a work by Dostoevsky in which the paradigm of child molestation does not occur. (It is an intriguing biographical detail that even as he was composing part 6 of *Crime and Punishment* Dostoevsky was becoming romantically involved with a woman twenty-six years his junior. He was forty-six and Anna Snitkin, the stenographer he hired and whom he married soon after, was twenty. In Dostoevsky's construction of his moral system, and in his selection of child molestation as the symbol of the ultimate evil, he may be reacting to a sense of guilt over proclivities he finds within himself.)

There is nothing overtly aggressive in Svidrigailov's attraction to little girls; he is a benevolent pedophile. But there is unquestionably more than avuncular affection in his delight at having his young fiancée sit on his lap, as he tells Raskolnikov (6:4):

> I sat her down on my knee yesterday, yes, quite unceremoniously, it must have been—she became quite flushed and little tears gleamed in her eyes, but she didn't want to betray how excited she was. But when everyone else left the room for a moment, as soon as we were left alone, she suddenly throws herself on my neck (it was the first time she had done this herself [this gesture is repeated in "Stavrogin's Confession"]), embraces me with both little hands, kisses me and swears, that she will be obedient, . . . that she will sacrifice [this word has the same root as the word for "victim"] everything. . . . You'll have to agree that listening to such a confession, alone, from such a little 16-year-old cherub, blushing with virginal embarrassment, and with tears of enthusiasm in her eyes—you'll have to agree that it's fairly alluring.

Raskolnikov responds with indignation that is apparently genuine, "this monstrous difference of age and development even aroused your sexual appetites! Do you really plan to marry her?" "What do you mean?" replies Svidrigailov. "'You bet I do. . . . And you, you've ridden onto the field of honor [literally, "with a big pole"] in the defense of virtue? Have mercy, little father, I'm a sinful man,' [Svidrigailov] ended laughing."

It is in Svidrigailov's dreams, just before his suicide at the end of chapter 6, that all of this comes to a head. I have noted that these dreams take place in a room very like the one in which Raskolnikov lives, and dreams.[40] There are three of them; the first is simply a "warm-up" in which he imagines that a mouse is crawling on his body under the sheets, a fantasy that is both disgusting and vaguely suggestive of sexuality. The second dream is of a drowned girl, a suicide. In the dream we learn that Svidrigailov knew her and that her suicide was the result of an outraged conscience, outraged most likely by rape or seduction. Luzhin has told us (4:2) that Svidrigailov has caused a young girl's suicide in much the same way, although her method was hanging. But this dream of the drowned girl has another echo as well—it reminds us of Afrosinya's attempted suicide in 2:6, which prompted Raskolnikov, who was standing on the bridge, to turn away from the idea of killing himself.

The third dream also begins as a real event and is very closely connected with the system of imagery relating to Raskolnikov's alternation between charitable and aggressive acts. In this dream Svidrigailov sees a battered female child, a victim needing rescue (and the child is wet, reminding us of the drowned girl of dream 2). One critic notes that the words that are used for the introduction of this child ("in a dark corner, between an old cupboard and the door, he made out a strange object, something that seemed to be alive") echo this passage from Raskolnikov's dream in 3:6: "in the corner, between a small cupboard and the window, he made out something like a cloak hanging on the wall. . . . He approached very quietly, feeling someone might be hiding behind the cloak." In Svidrigailov's dream, it is the drowned girl; in Raskolnikov's, it is the murdered pawnbroker, followed by the appearance of Svidrigailov after the dream ends.[41] This establishes for the reader a connection between the object of charity and the object of aggression. In any case, Svidrigailov's response to the battered child is the same as Raskolnikov's would be—he ministers to the child's needs, undressing her, drying her off, and putting her to bed. Svidrigailov being Svidrigailov, he must surely be aroused by this activity, although we are not told so, and he apparently does not take advantage of the situation. Perhaps because this is *his* dream, the connection between his charitable impulses and his sexual ones are repressed until the revelation a moment later. But the connection does become devastatingly, disgustingly clear at the climax of the dream, when the girl undergoes a metamorphosis and becomes a leering, inviting whore. Everything crystallizes for Svidrigailov: the victimized child, the object of brutal treatment, is equivalent to the female sexual object, therefore the sexually aggressive male is equivalent to a brutal aggressor, and sex equals aggression. This is exactly the connection that is posited for Raskolnikov in the symbolic scheme of the novel.

It is not this realization that makes Svidrigailov decide to take his life; he has obviously been planning suicide for some time. But this realization does elicit disgust and self-loathing, apparently for the first time, where earlier he had only taken delight in his own kinkiness. So why does Svidrigailov commit suicide? Perhaps he is disgusted, but perhaps he is simply tired of life. He has followed his own particular path to its end, and there is nowhere left to go but "to America," under the waters, to the spidery steambath in the sky.

There is one corollary of Svidrigailov's dream equation that he does not see. If sex equals aggression or murder, then birth equals resurrection. Svidrigailov does not see this, but Raskolnikov does. That is why they take different paths. That is Svidrigailov must shoot himself while Raskolnikov can go to Siberia with Sonya and begin the long and painful process of resurrection through suffering.

## CONFESSION

At the close of his meeting with Dunya in 6:7, Raskolnikov exclaims, "Oh I knew that I was a good-for-nothing standing on the Neva at dawn this morning." If he was listening closely while he was standing there, he must have heard a shot, for at that very moment

## Part 6

Svidrigailov was standing on the other side of the same river shooting himself. The time and place are mentioned so that we will make the connection. And in the epilogue, Raskolnikov's self-flagellation is even more closely connected with Svidrigailov's suicide: "he could not even do *that*."

Why does he call himself a "good-for-nothing"? Earlier in his conversation with his sister, he said that his whole project failed because of his "faintheartedness," "baseness," and "lack of talent." On his way to the police station he adds to this the adjectives, "insignificant" and "beggarly." All of these words suggest a sense of failure, not of guilt. Although he is about to confess, he is not repentant. Indeed, the very fact that he feels compelled to confess despite his lack of guilt feelings is a dramatic illustration of the failure of the crime to prove him special.

He visits Sonya and dons his cross, as planned, then sets out for the police station. His peculiar behavior prompts passersby to suggest that he is a pilgrim on his way to Jerusalem, and the narrator calls his walk a *via dolorosa (skorbnoe shestvie)*. One critic has noted that his path is the reverse of his path in chapter 1; the symmetry is carefully plotted.[42] Likewise, it has been pointed out that his first trip to the station turns out to be a "rehearsal," as he cannot bring himself to confess after hearing about Svidrigailov's suicide. Just as the murder is rehearsed in 1:1, so the confession is rehearsed in 6:8. But he does return (Sonya's eyes force him back in) and he does confess. The narrator uses his matter-of-fact tone for the confession; this tone is more effective than romantic exclamations when Dostoevsky wants to achieve the maximum in reader goose bumps.

# 10

# The Epilogue

The epilogue to *Crime and Punishment* has stirred up a good deal of controversy; in fact, it is probably the most controversial aspect of the novel. Regardless of one's position (both sides make some telling points) an understanding of the issues involved will deepen one's understanding of the novel as a whole.

The very existence of an epilogue implies that what has gone before is in important respects a completed aesthetic whole. An epilogue is supposed to tie up loose ends, to resolve threads of the plot that would otherwise be left dangling, after the completion of the aesthetic structure. But the final moment of the epilogue of this novel reverses, some would say negates or gives the lie to, essential elements of what has preceded it. The epilogue's detractors complain that Dostoevsky waves his Christian magic wand on the last page of the novel and all of the pathological elements of Raskolnikov's difficult personality vanish in a conversion that is wholly lacking in psychological credibility. Worse yet, they argue, Dostoevsky shirks his duty as a novelist to give us some details about Raskolnikov's new life after his conversion, a duty that could not be fulfilled anyway, since the phoniness of the whole thing would become immediately obvious. These readers are

# The Epilogue

irritated by the offhand shrug that defers the depiction of the good Raskolnikov's life to another novel in the final sentences of the epilogue. No, they object, this phony epilogue is already the new novel; *Crime and Punishment* ended with the confession of 6:8.

The defenders of the epilogue point to the symbolic preparation for the conversion in the emphasis on resurrection (rebirth, Lazarus, the New Jerusalem, and so forth) in the body of the novel. The details of life after the conversion are not given, they argue, simply because a good life lacks the conflict and drama necessary for an engaging work of literature. One may also note that the passages of reminiscence narration in the novel proper (e.g., "it seemed to him later that . . .") prepare us for the epilogue.[43]

Essentially, it all comes down to whether or not you believe in the validity of the religious experience of conversion or spiritual rebirth. Examples of genuine conversion are well documented in the literature on religious psychology; there is no reason Raskolnikov could not have such a conversion. The imagery of the novel really does point in that direction. Religiously inclined readers, particularly Christian readers, tend to agree with Dostoevsky's belief system and accept the epilogue. Readers with a psychological bent, interested in the novel's portrayal of an alienated personality, generally are unhappy with the epilogue. This group has included most of the existentialist movement of the mid-twentieth century (minus its Christian contingent) that has prized Dostoevsky for his brilliant diagnosis of modern man's alienation, but remained unconvinced by his tendency to locate the solution of the problem in traditional Christian theology. Whichever position one takes, wrestling with this idea is an invigorating experience, both intellectually and aesthetically, and brings us close to the heart of the novel's concerns.

This brings us back to the idea of polyphony. Both of the conflicting attitudes toward the epilogue seem to be characteristic of the text at different points. I have defined polyphony as the tendency to give opposing points of view equal credibility and comparable status in the work. And we have noted that polyphony is often related to an unresolved tension between opposing ideas within a character. Couldn't we be dealing here with a sort of metapolyphony on the (implied) authorial level, an unresolved tension between opposing ideas within the (implied) author?

Now readers unfamiliar with developments in literary criticism during the last three decades will not immediately understand the reason for including that parenthetical "implied" along with "author." Let us pause for a moment to define this term; it's one that will help us in the long run. It is useful to distinguish the authorial stance of a novel both from the narrator, the fictional voice whose actual words tell the story, and from the author in real life, the man of letters who also exercises bodily functions, has a family, and so forth. To take an obvious example from the tradition most readers are familiar with, the narrator of *Huckleberry Finn* is Huck. He is also the major character; he speaks in dialect and he has a rather limited understanding of the events he himself is telling us about. The implied author of the novel is "Mark Twain," who had a specific set of aesthetic purposes in writing the novel. Samuel Clemens, on the other hand, was a man of letters who created both the fictional character Huck Finn and the fictional novelist Mark Twain.

It is not always so easy to draw the distinction. In the work of Dostoevsky's greatest Russian contemporaries, Tolstoy and Turgenev, for instance, or in the work of a novelist like George Eliot, we may say that the implied author narrates the work, and since the goals change little from one work to another, the implied author of a given work is virtually indistinguishable from the novelist in real life. This is far from being the case with Dostoevsky.

We have already seen that *Crime and Punishment* is narrated by a disembodied quasi-magical intellect that sees into Raskolnikov's mind and presents the events of his mental life to us in the third person. We have also seen that the implied author of *Crime and Punishment* is an extraordinary psychologist with a compelling view of the workings of the human mind that was quite new for its time, and with a tragic understanding of the alienation of modern man driven by ideas to commit self-destructive acts.

Dostoevsky the man had an answer for the questions posed by

# The Epilogue

Dostoevsky the novelist. That answer was traditional Christianity. To be sure, he went from the moderate liberalism of his youth to the reactionary conservatism of the years during which he wrote all of his great novels, and in fact 1866, the year *Crime and Punishment* was written, may be called a transitional year for his faith. Still, it is accurate to say that Dostoevsky was always Christian, or more precisely, that he always had a faith based on the aesthetic beauty of the person of Jesus Christ. But Dostoevsky the novelist never allowed Dostoevsky the Christian to step in and make the novels into sermons. The Christian voice of Dostoevsky the man is always present, and always ready to step into the pulpit, but Dostoevsky the novelist never lets him do so. Well, seldom, anyway. This is even clearer in novels like *The Idiot* and *The Brothers Karamazov*. In *The Idiot* there is clearly a wish to see the Christ-like Myshkin as a totally redemptive figure. But Dostoevsky's artistic sensibility would not allow this didactic view to take over. In *The Brothers Karamazov* there is a clear preference for the self-denying Christianity of Alyosha Karamazov and Father Zosima over the intellectual doubts of his brother Ivan and Ivan's fictional Grand Inquisitor, but the two points of view battle it out on roughly equal terms, and the unresolved tension gives the book much of its intellectual vibrancy. To use Bakhtin's terminology, Dostoevsky the novelist remains poised in dialogue; he will not finalize himself with a decision as Dostoevsky the man did. To use existential terminology, Dostoevsky the novelist remains poised in becoming; while Dostoevsky the man made the leap of faith into being—being a Christian.

For Dostoevsky the novelist, art involves unresolved tension. A resolution of the tension, a decision to be this or that particular thing, is the destruction of art for Dostoevsky the novelist. Dostoevsky the man did make such a decision—he decided to be a Christian, monarchist, nongambling husband and father, and he seems to have made that decision at about the time he wrote *Crime and Punishment*. Dostoevsky the novelist, however, could still be a murderer, a nihilist, a pervert. Freud said that a novelist's various characters are fragments of the author's ego, hypothetical selves that are projected into the world in fictional embodiments. In Dostoevsky those fictionalized selves speak with an independence and "authority" that challenges the author himself, at least in his actual human incarnation. The characters seem to take over the prose and behave quite independently of the author.

Shakespeare's Shylock, in *The Merchant of Venice*, offers a clue. Shakespeare sets out to create a nice little comic villain in a stereotypical mode, but the character becomes bigger than that. Shylock arouses sympathies that cannot be dealt with in the play, because of what must happen to Shylock in the play. After all, he cannot really be allowed to cut Antonio's heart out onstage or off—it's just not that sort of play. But neither can the audience be satisfied by the dismissal of his legitimate complaints. Shylock is bigger than *The Merchant of Venice*. After his downfall, the play's well-made ending is a confusing anticlimax to a modern audience.

Likewise Dostoevsky. He creates characters who *must* be proven wrong. But since we see the world of those characters from inside, they arouse sympathies that are completely out of proportion with the feeling we would naturally have toward them as social stereotypes. Furthermore, those characters raise questions for which pat answers simply will not suffice. Thus any neat, moralistic endings are unsatisfying. The characters, and the questions they raise, are bigger than the novels. What we remember of *Crime and Punishment* disregards the epilogue.

This is the truth of polyphony; it is almost certainly not a conscious device for Dostoevsky. It is a function of the strength of the characters he created. They have a strength that challenges the authority of the novelist himself. It is the authority of the implied author, the embodiment of the artistic goals of the work itself, that keeps either from overcoming the other.

If we look at the actual text of the epilogue, we find that, through most of it, Raskolnikov's antisocial impulses are in the ascendancy. His behavior reminds us of those periods, early on in the novel, when he was leaning toward the murder, or away from confession, when he shunned human contact, treated his friends and family abruptly and rudely, when he felt that his actions were determined rather than free. He feels no real repentance. In thinking about the murder, he feels more than anything a sense of failure of the will. He feels that he was not strong enough to bring it off and that he has proven himself to be in that second, larger portion of humanity, the sheep-like masses who lack the moral strength to overstep boundaries. He contemplates Svidrigailov's suicide and wonders why he did not have the courage to take that path. He arouses the antipathy of his fellow convicts by his surliness, and he treats Sonya, whom they adore, with offhand cruelty. At one point they try to kill him, supposedly because they have decided that he is an atheist, although he has never discussed religion with them. In fact, much of this material was probably autobiographical. Dostoevsky was a misfit and a loner during his prison years in Siberia; he got along neither with the other political prisoners, who were Polish (a group he never liked), nor with the civil criminals, who were separated from him by class boundaries. Yet despite his inability to get along with the peasant convicts, he admired their strength of character and folk piety. This feature of his prison experience left its mark on his later work. His social philosophy of the 1860s, *pochven-nichestvo* or "soil-ism" (perhaps "grass roots-ism" is a happier formulation in English), was aimed at bridging the gap between the aristocracy and the peasant masses. His idealization of folk religiosity in later life seems to have been based on qualities he discovered among the peasants during his Siberian experience. It has been argued that the whole doctrine of the special person, who can overstep boundaries to commit crime without pangs of conscience, was based on types he encountered among his fellow convicts, and that he always harbored a negative evaluation of his own aristocratic, intellectual, indecisive self for lacking that sort of strength of character.[44] Be that as it may, much of the epilogue, particularly Raskolnikov's inability to fit in with his fellow prisoners, seems to be autobiographical.

This surly behavior continues through the dream sequence in the hospital, surely the most interesting section of the epilogue from a literary and psychological point of view:

> In his sickness he dreamed that the whole world was condemned to fall victim to some sort of horrible, unheard-of and never-before-seen fatal plague, which was proceeding out of the depths of Asia

into Europe. Everyone would perish except certain people, a very few chosen ones. Some sort of trichinae appeared, microscopic creatures which would infect people's bodies. But these creatures were spirits, endowed with intellect and will. Once they had taken these creatures into their bodies, people would become possessed and insane right away. But never, never had people considered themselves so intelligent and so unshakeable in their knowledge of the truth as did these infected people.

The dream goes on to describe at length the mass-scale aggression that this intellectual infection produces, finally concluding as follows: "The pestilence grew and moved further and further. The only people in the whole world who could save themselves were a few people, pure and chosen ones who had been predestined to found a new race of people and a new life, to renew and purify the earth, but no one had ever seen these people anywhere; no one had ever heard their words and their voices."

It is a dream about aggression for the sake of ideas, and as such it is a fitting epilogue to the novel and prologue to the twentieth-century. It takes some of the aspects of Raskolnikov's individual intellectual aggression and sketches them out on a social and international canvas, showing how the same aggressive paradigms operate on the level of intergroup relations.

But the intellectual aggression that is described could as easily be religious dogmatism as any kind of godless ideology. Indeed, the one example of idea-based aggression in the epilogue is the convicts' attack on Raskolnikov, which is carried out because they suppose him to be an atheist. The idea of men killing each other for ideas could easily describe the Balkan wars of Dostoevsky's own day, when his own beloved pan-Slavism, and the opposing forces of Islam, were the idea microbes for which men killed one another. Most examples of idea-based aggression prior to the twentieth century have been religiously motivated. In fact, the word *zaráz* ("infection"), one of the words used for the idea-microbes in the epilogue, has been used earlier in the novel to describe the transmission of religious ideas from Sonya and Lizaveta to Raskolnikov ("They're religious maniacs [yuródivye]! You'll become one yourself here—it's infectious! [zarazítelno] he thought to himself" [4:4]).

If we look at the "anthropology" of the dream, we can see that, like Raskolnikov's theory on crime, this dream divides humanity into a large contemptible mass, those infected with the microbe, and a small elite, the chosen few who are predestined to renew the world. Indeed, the elite's crusade to "cleanse" the earth is also an "idea"— could it not cause the same sort of destruction as the "idea-microbes"? In fact these details of the dream link up with the image system of the novel in a way that is precisely the opposite of what we would expect from the Christian perspective that is introduced a page or so later. The fact is that up until this point the narrator of the epilogue has not committed himself to a particular ideology or religious system.

Shortly after this dream comes the conversion, which occupies only the last couple of pages of the novel, with all of its magical elements and stock happy-ending devices. At least some attempt is made to connect it with the murder and the confession to Sonya, through imagery. We are told that he reached for the New Testament "mechanically," an image that was repeated almost obsessively in those earlier scenes. The conversion is closely tied to the person of Sonya and to her moral beauty, just as Dostoevsky's commitment to Christianity was a devotion to the person of Christ, to his overwhelming aesthetic and moral beauty, rather than to theological principles as such.

Might we not say that we have two separate epilogues here: one belonging to the implied author, interested in the novel as a work of art, trying to tie together and conclude the system of images that forms the novel as a work of art; the other belonging to the real author, interested in a didactic, Christian ending. If we expand this idea to include the narrator, we might say that he dropped out at the end of 6:8, before the epilogue, since that is the last place where we had a detailed look at Raskolnikov's world through his own eyes, described by a third-person narrator. There is little attention to his inner life in the epilogue, except for the first few pages of the second chapter. It has been argued that the body of the novel (parts 1–6) is a classical tragedy while the epilogue makes it a Christian rebirth myth.[45]

Each author figure has his own ending. For the narrator it is the confession at the crossroads—abrupt and shocking, even though expected. This ends the novel with a powerful jolt, and this is the ending we remember. The implied author then tells us what happened to Dunya, Razumikhin, and Mrs. Raskolnikov, concentrating on the last, and shows us Raskolnikov's and Sonya's fully characteristic behavior in Siberia. This implied author ends with the microbe dream, a powerful outline of the workings of intellectually driven aggression, the subject of the novel, on the level of group behavior. This author figure ends by panning back and making panoramic what had been individual. The third author figure, Dostoevsky himself, steps on stage in the final moments and shows us Raskolnikov's conversion. It is a trifle saccharine, to be sure, and irritatingly offhand about important details. But it is fully credible, given what we know about the psychology of the conversion experience in religion, and quite consistent, even prepared for, in terms of the image system of the novel itself. None of these endings is wrong. They are simply different. These three endings represent the distinct points of view of these three distinguishable author figures: the narrator, the implied author, and the actual author.

*Crime and Punishment* really did represent a watershed in Dostoevsky's career as a novelist, as in his personal life. Perhaps that is why the polyphony is so strongly felt at the authorial level. It was his first full-length novel of unquestionable greatness. It was his first attempt to find a positive answer to the psychological problems posed in *Notes from Underground*. It was the first work strongly characterized by polyphony, perhaps because the greater tranquillity of his personal life allowed him to project the demons that tormented him into works of literature.

# Appendix: List of Characters

In Russian a person may be addressed or referred to by nickname (intimate), first name (slightly less intimate), first name *plus* middle name (formal but friendly), or last name (emotionally neutral). Some translators, trying to avoid confusion, will use last name throughout, even when the Russian text uses first name and patronymic. Do not worry if your translation gives a different form of the name than the one used in quotations in this book, as long as the same person is being talked about.

For the most part names of characters who are only mentioned but never seen (for example, Chebárov, Dárya Fránzevna, Kheruvímov), or who are seen but never named (for example, Svidrigáilov's fiancée, the funeral guests), are omitted here, because their identity is always made clear by the context.

Raskólnikov, Rodión Románovich—former student (*raskól*, "schism," "split").

Raskólnikov, Pulkhériya Alexándrovna—his mother.

Raskólnikov, Avdótya Románovna (Dúnya)—his sister.

Praskóvya Pávlovna Zarnítsyn (Páshenka)—his landlady, whose late daughter Raskólnikov almost married the year before.

Nastásya Petróvna—her servant.

Razumíkhin, Dmítri Prokófich—Raskólnikov's friend, also a former student (*razum*, "sense," "intelligence"). He puns on his own name, calling himself "Vrazumíkhin"; the added prefix makes the name suggest "to bring someone to his senses."

Zosímov—a friend of Razumíkhin and Raskólnikov, a young doctor (Zosíma is the name of a saint in the Russian/Greek Orthodox tradition).

Lúzhin, Peter Petróvich—Dúnya Raskólnikov's fiancé, a self-important social climber, intellectual poseur, corrupt lawyer (*luzha*, "puddle").

Svidrigáilov, Arkády Ivánovich—a landowner, neighbor of the Raskólnikovs in the country; formerly employed Dunya as a governess (Arkády suggests "Arcadia").

Svidrigáilov, Márfa Petróvna—his late wife.

Alyóna Ivánovna—an old woman who runs a pawnshop out of her apartment.

Lizavéta Ivánovna—her half-sister.

Marmeládov, Semyón Zakhárych—an out-of-work alcoholic, formerly a low-grade bureaucrat (*marmelád*, "marmelade").

Marmeládov, Katerína Ivánovna—his consumptive wife.

Marmeládov, Sofía Semyónovna (Sónya)—his daughter, a prostitute (Russian, Greek, *sofia*, "wisdom," "spiritual knowledge").

Pólenka, Lída, others—the Marmeládov children.

Líppewechsel, Amália Ivánovna (or Fyódorovna, or Ludwígovna)—their German landlady (German, *Líppe*, "lip,"; *Wéchsel*, "change")./

Lebezyátnikov, Andréi Semyónovich—another resident at Frau Líppewechsel's, with left-wing political tendencies (*lebezít*, "to cringe").

Nikodím Fomích—the supervisor of the police station in Raskólnikov's precinct.

Ilyá Petróvich—a hot-tempererd police lieutenant.

Zamétov—the precinct clerk (his name suggests either "to sweep behind," in which case pronounced "Zamyótov," or "to notice," in which case pronounced "Zamétov").

Porfíry Petróvich—a detective (an unusual name in Russian, suggesting the semi-precious stone, porphyry).

Luíza (Lavíza) Ivánovna—another German landlady, of questionable reputation; a petitioner at the station.

Résslich—a German madam and landlady; friend of Svidrigáilov, to whom she lets a flat; also lets to the Kapernaúmovs ("Capernaums"), who sublet a room to Sónya.

# Appendix: List of Characters

Koch—another customer of Alyóna Ivánovna, the pawnbroker.

Pestryakóv—another customer.

Mítka—a house painter, working in Alyóna Ivánovna's building.

Nikolái (Mikólka)—another house painter.

Mikólka—a peasant who beats a horse in Raskólnikov's dream.

Vakhrúshin, Afanásy Ivánovich—a friend of the Raskólnikov family, through whom Pulkhériya Aleksándrovna sends money to Raskólnikov.

# Notes

1. Viacheslav Ivanov, *Freedom and the Tragic Life* (New York: Noonday Press, 1957), 77–78.

2. Nicholas Berdyaev, *Dostoevsky* (New York: Meridian Books, 1957), 99–101.

3. J. M. Murry, *Dostoevsky* (London: Martin Secker, 1923), 127.

4. D. H. Lawrence, *The Quest for Ra Na Nim* (Montreal: McGill-Queens University Press, 1970), 102–3.

5. Lawrence, *Quest*, 37.

6. Albert Camus, *The Myth of Sisyphus and Other Essays* (New York: Knopf, 1955), 104.

7. Richard Rosenthal, "Raskolnikov's Transgression and the Confusion between Destructiveness and Creativity," in *Do I Dare Disturb the Universe*, ed. James Grotstein (Beverly Hills, Calif.: Caesura Press, 1981), 200.

8. See J. M. Meijer, "Situation Rhyme in a Novel of Dostoevsky," in *Dutch Contributions to the 4th International Congress of Slavists* (The Hague: Mouton, 1958), 115–29; James Curtis, "Spatial Form as the Intrinsic Genre of Dostoevsky's Novels," *Modern Fiction Studies* 18, no. 2 (Summer 1972): 135–54; Ralph Matlaw, "Recurrent Imagery in Dostoevsky," *Harvard Slavic Studies* 3 (1957): 201–25.

9. See Rosenthal, "Raskolnikov's Transgression."

10. See Gary Rosenshield, *"Crime and Punishment": The Techniques of the Omniscient Author* (Lisse: Peter De Ridder Press, 1978); Julia Kristeva,

# Notes

"The Ruin of a Poetics," in *Russian Formalism*, ed. S. Bann and J. Bowlt (Edinburgh: Scottish Academic Press, 1973), 102–21; Michael Holquist, *Dostoevsky and the Novel* (Princeton: Princeton University Press, 1977); Wolf Schmid, Der Textaufbau in den Erzählungen Dostoevskijs (Munich: Wilhelm Fink Verlag, 1973).

11. A. L. Bem, *Psikhoanaliticheskie etyudy* (Prague: Petropolis, 1938), 41.

12. Gary Rosenshield, *"Crime and Punishment": Techniques*, 50.

13. Malcolm Jones, *Dostoevsky: The Novel of Discord* (New York: Barnes and Noble, 1976), 17.

14. Konstantin Mochulsky, *Dostoevsky: His Life and Work* (Princeton: Princeton University Press, 1967), 278–89.

15. R. L. Jackson, *Dostoevsky's Quest for Form* (Bloomington, Ind.: Physsardt Publishers, 1978), 84–85.

16. A. L. Bem, "Gogol i Pushkin v tvorchestve Dostoevskogo," *Slavia* 7, no. 8 (1930):82–100.

17. N. G. Chernyshevsky, *What Is to Be Done?*, 3:29, "An Extraordinary Person."

18. James Curtis, "Spatial Form," 152–53.

19. Jackson, *Dostoevsky's Quest*, 98–99.

20. Bem, "Gogol i Pushkin," 82–100.

21. Mikhail Bakhtin, *Problems of Dostoevsky's Poetics* (Ann Arbor, Mich.: Ardis, 1973), 4.

22. Robert Lord, *Dostoevsky: Essays and Perspectives* (London: Chatto and Windus, 1970), 201.

23. Bakhtin, *Dostoevsky's Poetics*, 51.

24. Ibid., 52.

25. See Rosenshield, *"Crime and Punishment": Techniques*, 29.

26. Philip Rahv, "Dostoevsky in *Crime and Punishment*," in *Dostoevsky: A Collection of Critical Essays*, ed. René Welleck (Englewood Cliffs, N.J.: Prentice-Hall, 1962), 542.

27. Bakhtin, *Dostoevsky's Poetics*, 52.

28. Edward Wasiolek, *The Notebooks for "Crime and Punishment"* (Chicago: University of Chicago Press, 1967), 187.

29. See Wasiolek, *Notebooks*, 96, 165.

30. Bem, *Psikhoanaliticheskie etyudy*, 45.

31. Ernest Simmons, *Dostoevsky: The Making of a Novelist* (New York: Random House, 1940), 161–62; R. P. Blackmur, "*Crime and Punishment*: Murder in Your Own Room," in *Eleven Essays in the European Novel* (New York: Harcourt, Brace & World, 1964), 119–40.

32. Lord, *Dostoevsky*, 218.

33. Richard Rosenthal, "Raskolnikov's Transgression," 222.

34. Bem, *Psikhoanaliticheskie etyudy*, 180–86.

35. J. M. Meijer. "Situation Rhyme," 115–29; Ralph Matlaw, "Recurrent Imagery in Dostoevsky," 201–25; Curtis, "Spatial Form," 135–54.

36. Curtis, "Spatial Form," 146–47; W. D. Snodgrass, "Crime for Punishment: The Tenor of Part One," *Hudson Review* 13 (1960): 219.

37. Curtis, "Spatial Form," 146–47.

38. Maurice Beebe, "Three Motives of Raskolnikov," in *Crime and Punishment* (New York: Norton, 1975), 585–96.

39. Pearl Niemi, "The Art of *Crime and Punishment*," *Modern Fiction Studies* 9 (1964): 304.

40. Edward Wasiolek, "Structure and Detail," in *"Crime and Punishment" and the Critics*, ed. E. Wasiolek (Belmont, Calif.: Wadsworth Publishing Company, 1961), 114.

41. Erik Krag, *Dostoevsky: The Literary Artist* (New York: Humanities Press, 1962), 124.

42. Richard Gill, "The Bridges of St. Petersburg: A Motif in *Crime and Punishment*," *Dostoevsky Studies* 3 (1982): 152.

43. Rosenshield, *"Crime and Punishment": Techniques*, 107–8.

44. Lev Shestov, *Dostoevsky, Tolstoy, and Nietzsche* (Athens: Ohio University Press, 1969), 211–12.

45. Steven Cassedy, "The Formal Problem of the Epilogue in *Crime and Punishment*," *Dostoevsky Studies* 3 (1982): 171–90.

# Selected Bibliography

## Primary Works

The definitive source in Russian is the new *Polnoe sobranie sochinenii* (Complete collected works) currently in publication by the Soviet Academy of Sciences. Thirty volumes are projected, and all but the last few (containing letters written during the last years of the author's life) are now in print. Dates vary, but the project was begun in 1972. *Prestuplenie i nakazanie* (Crime and punishment) is in volume 6, with a date of 1977. The notebooks for this novel are in volume 7.

## Novels, Stories, and Nonfiction

This list of Dostoevsky's major works is arranged chronologically. Most of these works exist in several good editions, and some of these choices are arbitrary. Where possible, preference has been given to works currently in print, and to the translations of the most established translators, such as Constance Garnett, Jessie Coulson, and David Magarshack.

*Poor Folk* (1846). Translated by Robert Dessaix. Ann Arbor, Michigan: Ardis Publishers, 1982.

*The Double* (1846). Translated by Jessie Coulson. New York: Penguin, 1972. Bound with *Notes from Underground*.

"The Landlady" (1847). Translated by Constance Garnett. Pp. 248–318 in *The Gambler and other Stories*. New York: Macmillan, 1950.

*White Nights* (1848). Translated by Constance Garnett. New York: Macmillan, 1950.

*Netochka Nezvanova* (1849). Translated by Jane Kentish. New York: Penguin, 1986.

*Uncle's Dream* (1859). Translated by Constance Garnett. Pp. 223–342 in *The Short Novels of Dostoevsky*. New York: Dial Press, 1945.

*The Friend of the Family* (translation of *The Village of Stepanchikovo and Its Inhabitants*, 1859). Translated by Constance Garnett. Pp. 617–811 in *The Short Novels of Dostoevsky*. New York: Dial Press, 1945. Some English editions use Dostoevsky's original title.

*Memoirs from the House of the Dead* (1860). Translated by Jessie Coulson. Oxford: Oxford University Press, 1983.

*The Insulted and the Injured* (1861). Translated by Constance Garnett. Westport, Conn.: Greenwood Press, 1975.

*Winter Notes on Summer Impressions* (1863). Translated by Kyril Fitzlyon. London: Quartet Books, 1985.

*Notes from Underground* (1864). Translated by Jessie Coulson. New York: Penguin, 1972. Bound with *The Double*.

*The Gambler* (1866). Translated by Jessie Coulson. New York: Penguin, 1966.

*Crime and Punishment* (1866). Translated by Jessie Coulson; revised edition by George Gibian. Norton Critical Editions. New York: W. W. Norton, 1975. Other recommended editions include translations by Constance Garnett (New York: Bantam, 1984), David Magarshack (New York: Penguin, 1952), and Sidney Monas (New York: New American Library, 1968).

*The Idiot* (1868). Translated by Constance Garnett. New York: Bantam, 1987.

*The Eternal Husband* (1870). Translated by Constance Garnett. Pp. 343–474 in *The Short Novels of Dostoevsky*. New York: Dial Press, 1945.

*The Devils* (1871). Translated by David Magarshack. New York: Penguin, 1954. Garnett and others have translated this work under the title *The Possessed*.

*A Raw Youth* (1875). Translated by Constance Garnett. New York: Dial Press, 1947. Others have translated this work under the title *The Adolescent*.

*The Diary of a Writer* (1873–81). Translated by Boris Brasol. New York: George Braziller, 1954.

"A Gentle Creature" (1871). Translated by Constance Garnett. Pp. 285–323

# Selected Bibliography

in *The Eternal Husband and Other Stories*. New York: Macmillan, 1950. This work has been translated under a variety of titles, including "The Meek One," "A Gentle Spirit," and "A Meek Girl."

"The Dream of a Ridiculous Man" (1877). Translated by Olga Shartse. Pp. 201–20 in *From Karamzin to Bunin: An Anthology of Russian Short Stories*, edited by Carl Proffer. Bloomington: Indiana University Press, 1969. Other translations of this title include "A Strange Man's Dream."

*The Brothers Karamazov* (1879–80). Translated by Constance Garnett; revised edition by Ralph Matlaw. Norton Critical Editions. New York: W. W. Norton, 1950.

For a good collection of shorter works, see also David Magarshack, translator, *The Best Short Stories of Dostoevsky*. New York: Modern Library, 1964.

## Memoirs

Dostocvsky, Aimee (Lyubov [daughter]). *Fyodor Dostoevsky*. New Haven: Yale University Press, 1922.

Dostoevsky, Anna (wife). *Dostoevsky: Reminiscences*. New York: Liveright, 1975.

## Collections of Letters

Coulson, Jessie, Ed. *Dostoevsky: A Self Portrait*. Westport, Conn.: Greenwood Press, 1962.

Frank, Joseph, and David Goldstein, eds. *Selected Letters of Fyodor Dostoevsky*. New Brunswick, N.J.: Rutgers University Press, 1987.

Lowe, David, and Ronald Meyer, trans. and eds. *Fyodor Dostoevsky: Complete Letters*. Ann Arbor: Ardis Publishers, 1988 (vol. 1), 1989 (vol. 2). Additional volumes forthcoming.

## Notebooks, Diaries, Marginalia

Kjetsaa, Keir. *Dostoevsky and His New Testament*. Atlantic Highlands, N.J.: Humanities Press, 1984.

Proffer, Carl, ed. *The Unpublished Dostoevsky: Diaries and Notebooks, (1860–1881)*. Vol. 1. Ann Arbor, Mich.: Ardis, 1973.

Wasiolek, Edward, ed. *The Notebooks for "Crime and Punishment."* Chicago:

University of Chicago Press, 1967. Wasiolek has a volume of translated notes out for each of Dostoevsky's major novels.

## Secondary Works

### Biographies

Carr, E. H. *Dostoevsky: A New Biography*. Boston, Houghton Mifflin, 1931. This was the first work to challenge Freud's view of the connection between parricide and epilepsy. Once considered the definitive biography, it is still usable.

Frank, Joseph. *Dostoevsky* 5 vols. Princeton: Princeton University Press, Vol. 1, 1976; Vol. 2, 1983; Vol. 3, 1986; Vols, 4 and 5 forthcoming. Definitive; discusses primary sources, critical issues, the creative process, connections between works. Some quirky critical views.

Grossman, Leonid P. *Dostoevskii: A Biography*, translated by Mary Mackler. Indianapolis: Bobbs-Merrill, 1975. The best Soviet critical biography; indispensible.

Magarshack, David. *Dostoevsky*. Westport, Conn.: Greenwood Press, 1975. A solid, intelligent biography, without all of Frank's detail on composition.

Mochulsky, Konstantin. *Dostoevsky: His Life and Work*. Princeton: Princeton University Press, 1967. Probably the best biography prior to Frank's.

Simmons, Ernest J. *Dostoevsky: The Making of a Novelist*. New York: Random House, Vintage Books, 1940. Gives much attention to the notebooks and the writing process.

### Critical Studies

Bakhtin, Mikhail. *Problems of Dostoevsky's Poetics*. Ann Arbor: Ardis Publishers, 1973. Introduces the concept of polyphony.

Berdyaev, Nicholas. *Dostoevsky*. Translated by Donald Atwater. New York: Meridian Books, 1957. This Russian Orthodox theologian bases his version of existentialism on Dostoevsky.

Berlin, Isaiah. "The Hedgehog and the Fox." In *Russian Thinkers*, 22–81. New York: Viking, 1978. Tolstoyan and Dostoevskian writers are contrasted.

Blackmur, R. P. "*Crime and Punishment*: Murder in Your Own Room." In

# Selected Bibliography

*Eleven Essays in the European Novel*, 119–40. New York: Harcourt, Brace & World, 1964. A classic.

Camus, Albert. *The Myth of Sisyphus and Other Essays*. Translated by Justin O'Brien. New York: Knopf, 1955. A classic of existentialism.

———. *The Stranger*. Translated by Stuart Gilbert. New York: Random House, 1954. No other work of twentieth-century fiction shows the influence of *Crime and Punishment* so clearly.

Cassedy, Steven. "The Formal Problem of the Epilogue in *Crime and Punishment*: The Logic of Tragic and Christian Structures." *Dostoevsky Studies* 3 (1982):171–90. Illuminating.

Chapple, Richard. *A Dostoevsky Dictionary*. Ann Arbor: Ardis Publishers, 1983. Compendium of characters, major and minor, and other data on all the novels. Helpful.

Cox, Gary. "Dostoevskian Psychology and Russian Political and Cultural Identity." *Mosaic: A Journal for the Interdisciplinary Study of Literature* 17, no. 3 (Summer 1984): 87–102. Applies Dostoevskian paradigms to contemporary culture.

———. *Tyrant and Victim in Dostoevsky*. Columbus, Ohio: Slavica Publishers, 1984. Inversion of dominance hierarchy as basic paradigm in Dostoevsky.

Curtis, James. "Spatial Form as the Intrinsic Genre of Dostoevsky's Novels." *Modern Fiction Studies* 18, no. 2 (Summer 1972): 135–54. Preoccupied with theoretical classifications, but does make some good points.

Fanger, Donald. *Dostoevsky and Romantic Realism*. Cambridge: Harvard University Press, 1967. Dostoevsky's debt to the urban, Gothic, proto-realism of Balzac, Dickens, and Gogol.

Forster, E. M. "Prophecy." In *Aspects of the Novel*, 86–101. London: Edward Arnold, 1974. The British novelist finds Dostoevsky and D. H. Lawrence similar in their "prophetic" character.

Garnett, Edward. "Dostoevsky." *Academy* 71 (1906):202–3. An early British appreciation of Dostoevsky.

Gibian, George. "Backgrounds and Sources" and "Essays in Criticism." In Norton Critical Edition of *Crime and Punishment* by Fyodor Dostoevsky. New York: W. W. Norton, 1975. The best collection, bound with the novel (Coulson translation). Includes Gibian's "Traditional Symbolism in *Crime and Punishment*," Philip Rahv's "Dostoevsky in *Crime and Punishment*," Maurice Beebe's "The Three Motives of Raskolnikov," and Ruth Mortimer's "Dostoevsky and the Dream," among other fine articles.

Gibson, A. Boyce. *The Religion of Dostoevsky*. Philadelphia: Westminster Press, 1973. A scholarly study of Christian themes in the novels.

Gide, André. *Dostoevsky*. New York: New Directions, 1961. Speeches on Dostoevsky by a major French writer who was indebted to him.

Gill, Richard. "The Bridges of St. Petersburg: A Motif in *Crime and Punishment.*" *Dostoevsky Studies* 3 (1982):145–55. Helpful.

Girard, René. *Deceit, Desire, and the Novel: Self and Other In Literary Structure.* Baltimore: Johns Hopkins Press, 1965. A basic study, but it concentrates more on the later works.

Grossman, Leonid. *Balzac and Dostoevsky.* Ann Arbor: Ardis Publishers, 1973. A classic study of sources by a leading Soviet specialist.

Holquist, Michael. *Dostoevsky and the Novel.* Princeton: Princeton University Press, 1977. Sees "history" as central reality in Dostoevsky.

Ivanov, Viacheslav. *Freedom and the Tragic Life.* New York: Noonday Press, 1957. Written by a symbolist poet who was also a classicist, this classic study mixes Greek tragedy and Christian mysticism.

Jackson, R. L. *Twentieth Century Interpretations of "Crime and Punishment."* Englewood Cliffs, N. J.: Prentice-Hall, 1974. Valuable for its translation of some Russian studies otherwise unavailable in English.

———. *Dostoevsky's Quest for Form: A Study of His Philosophy of Art.* N.p.: Physsardt, 1978. A fine study of Dostoevskian aesthetics.

Jones, Malcolm V. *Dostoevsky: The Novel of Discord.* New York: Barnes & Noble, 1976. Treats Dostoevsky as series of oppositions, revolving around chaos/order opposition.

Kaufmann, Walter. *Existentialism from Dostoevsky to Sartre.* New York: Meridian Books, 1956. Presents part 1 of *Notes from Underground* with a good introduction.

Krag, Erik. *Dostoevsky: The Literary Artist.* New York: Humanities Press, 1976. Very perceptive.

Kristeva, Julia. "The Ruin of a Poetics." In *Russian Formalism*, edited by S. Bann and John Bowlt, 102–21. Edinburgh: Scottish Academic Press, 1973. A poststructuralist Bakhtinian study.

Lary, N. M. *Dostoevsky and Dickens.* London: Routledge & Kegan Paul, 1973. Good comparative study.

Lawrence, D. H. *The Crown.* London: Signature, 1915. Always stimulating, if occasionally perverse.

———. *The Quest for Ra Na Nim: D. H. Lawrence's Letters to S. S. Koteliansky, 1914–1930.* Edited by G. J. Zytaruk. Montreal: McGill-Queens University Press, 1970.

Linner, Sven. *Dostoevskij on Realism.* Stockholm: Almqvist & Wiksell, 1967. Good on Dostoevskian aesthetics, but does not treat this novel at length.

Lord, Robert. *Dostoevsky: Essays and Perspectives.* London: Chatto & Windus, 1970. One of the best. Good on polyphony. Concentrates on the later novels.

# Selected Bibliography

Matlaw, Ralph. "Recurrent Imagery in Dostoevsky." *Harvard Slavic Studies* 3 (1957): 201–25. Namely, spiders and bugs.

Meijer, J. M. "Situation Rhyme in a Novel of Dostoevsky." In *Dutch Contributions, 4th International Congress of Slavists,* 115–29. The Hague: Mouton, 1958. The best study of one of Dostoevsky's central compositional techniques.

Merejkowski, Dmitri. *Tolstoi as Man and Artist, with an Essay on Dostoevsky.* Westminster, England: Archibald Constable & Co., 1902. Dostoevsky, seer of the spirit, contrasted with Tolstoy, seer of the flesh.

Mikhailovsky, Nikolai. *Dostoevsky: A Cruel Talent.* Ann Arbor: Ardis Publishers, 1978. An early classic; hostile but illuminating on the sadomasochistic complex.

Muchnic, Helen. *Dostoevsky's English Reputation. Smith College Studies in Modern Languages* 20, nos. 3–4 (April–July 1939). Good background on Dostoevsky's impact in the West.

Murry, J. Middleton. *Fyodor Dostoevsky: A Critical Study.* London: Martin Secker, 1923. A classic early English interpretation.

Niemi, Pearl. "The Art of *Crime and Punishment." Modern Fiction Studies* 9 (1964):291–313. One of the best articles.

Nuttall, A. D. *"Crime and Punishment": Murder as Philosophic Experiment.* Sussex, England: University of Sussex Press, 1978. Good on Svidrigailov.

Passage, Charles. *Character Names in Dostoevsky's Fiction.* Ann Arbor: Ardis Publishers, 1982. Everything you ever wanted to know on the subject, and more.

Roheim, G. "The Significance of Stepping Over." *International Journal of Psychoanalysis* 3 (1922):320–26. A psychoanalytic look at one of the novel's main devices.

Rosenshield, Gary. *"Crime and Punishment": Techniques of the Omniscient Author.* Lisse, The Netherlands: Peter de Ridder Press, 1978. A superb study of the narrative system. Essential.

Rosenthal, Richard. "Raskolnikov's Transgression and the Confusion between Destructiveness and Creativity." *Do I Dare Disturb the Universe: A Memorial to Wilfred R. Bion,* edited by James Grotstein, 197–235. Beverly Hills, Calif.: Caesura Press, 1981. A fine representative of the psychoanalytic literature on the novel.

Shaw, J. Thomas. "Raskolnikov's Dreams." *Slavic and East European Journal* 17 (1973):131–45. Perhaps the best study of the dreams.

Snodgrass, W. D. "Crime and Punishment: The Tenor of Part One." *Hudson Review* 13 (1960):202–53. Classic.

Wasiolek, Edward, ed. *"Crime and Punishment" and the Critics.* Belmont,

Calif.: Wadsworth Publishing Co., 1961. A fine casebook that covers all the bases. A bit dated (in terms of editions cited, biblography, etc.).

———. *Dostoevsky: The Major Fiction.* Cambridge, Mass.: MIT Press, 1964. Perhaps the best introduction in English to Dostoevsky's body of work.

Wellek, René. *Dostoevsky.* Englewood Cliffs, N.J.: Prentice-Hall, 1962. Collection includes classic essays by Freud, Rahv, Lukács, and Dmitri Chizhevsky.

Zander, L. A. *Dostoevsky.* London: SCM Press, 1948. A solid theological study by an expatriate Russian Orthodox theologian.

# Index

# Index

# About the Author

Gary Cox is associate professor of Russian literature and language at Southern Methodist University in Dallas, Texas, where he heads the Russian Area Studies Program. He received his B.A. in religion and philosophy from Earlham College (1969), his M.A. in Russian language and literature from Indiana University (1973), and his Ph.D. in Russian language and literature from Columbia University (1978). He has studied at Harvard and Moscow State universities and taught at the University of Missouri at Columbia before coming to SMU in 1981.

Cox is the author of *Tyrant and Victim in Dostoevsky*, which views the author's aesthetic, psychological, and ethical systems as versions of a paradigm involving inversion of a dominance hierarchy. He leads touring groups to the Soviet Union and participates in "citizen diplomacy" efforts to maximize grassroots contact between American and Soviet citizens. He directs students in Russian-language theatrical productions, acts as a consultant for professional English-language productions of Russian works, and is involved in community theater.